79p DIW

*The Pitman Motor-cyclists' Library*

The Book of the

# A.M.C. SINGLES

A Practical Guide to the Handling and Maintenance of 1955-66 O.H.V. A.J.S., Matchless and Norton Touring Singles

**W. C. Haycraft**

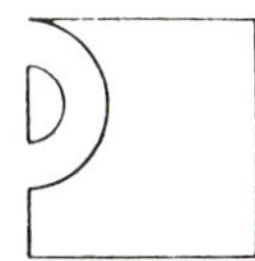

**Pitman Publishing**

*First Published* 1973

*Adapted from* The Book of the A.J.S., The Book of the Matchless
'The Book of the Norton

SIR ISAAC PITMAN AND SONS LTD.
Pitman House, Parker Street, Kingsway, London, WC2B 5PB
P.O. Box 46038, Portal Street, Nairobi, Kenya

SIR ISAAC PITMAN (AUST.) PTY. LTD.
Pitman House, 158 Bouverie Street, Carlton, Victoria 3053, Australia

PITMAN PUBLISHING COMPANY S.A. LTD.
P.O. Box 11231, Johannesburg, South Africa

PITMAN PUBLISHING CORPORATION
6 East 43rd Street, New York, N.Y. 10017, U.S.A.

SIR ISAAC PITMAN (CANADA) LTD.
495 Wellington Street West, Toronto 2B, Canada

THE COPP CLARK PUBLISHING COMPANY
517 Wellington Street West, Toronto 2B, Canada





ISBN: 0 273 31700 8

Text set in 8/9pt Monotype Times New Roman, printed by photo-lithography, and bound in Great Britain at The Pitman Press, Bath

G. 4256:19

# Preface

This handbook combines the three separate manuals previously published in this series on A.J.S., Matchless and Norton single-cylinder motor-cycles. From 1955–66 these three marques were in many cases identical save for their tank badges.

Thus Norton in this period included the 19 (596 c.c.), the ES2 (498 c.c.), and the 50 (348 c.c.). At the same time A.J.S. "badge" equivalents were the 348 c.c. 16/16S (Mercury/Mercury Sports), and the 498 c.c 18/18S (Statesman/Sceptre). There were Matchless models G3LS, G3S, G3, and the Majors—G80S, G80. The Mark II Nortons 348 and 498 also had their Matchless equals.

A.M.C.—Associated Motor Cycles—absorbed the separate concerns and the similarity between models at the dates stated enabled this book to be condensed from its predecessors. Today Norton Villiers Ltd., North Way, Walworth Industrial Estate, Andover, Hants, are responsible for Norton and A.J.S. machines, while spares for Burman gearboxes may be still available from Burman & Sons Ltd., Wychall Lane, Kings Norton, Birmingham 30.

Norton Villiers are again thanked for technical help and permission to reproduce copyright illustrations.

Since 1966 single-cylinder touring models of these makes have been discontinued. The *Book of the Norton Dominator Twins* continues as a separate volume.

# Contents

# 1 Handling Your Motor-cycle

This chapter is mainly for those who have had little or no previous motor-cycling experience. The handling of a motor-cycle is quickly mastered, the engine being very responsive, and all controls conveniently located and easy to operate.

First verify that there is sufficient petrol and oil in the tanks. Handlebar controls are shown in Fig. 1.; oil tank and gearbox replenishment are dealt with on pages 13 and 20 respectively. Check that the gear-change pedal *is* in neutral (*see* Figs. 2, 3).

**Setting the Engine Controls.** If the engine is cold—

1. Set the throttle so that it is slightly open by turning the twist-grip *inwards* about *one-sixth* of its total movement.

2. Completely close the air control lever.

3. Fully advance the ignition control (where fitted) by pushing it *outwards* to its *full extent*, and then retard it by about *two-fifths* of its total movement by pulling it *inwards*.

4. On 1958–66 models turn the ignition switch to the "ON" position.

If the engine is already warm, open the throttle about a quarter and the air-control lever half to three-quarters.

**Removing Petrol Tank Filler Cap.** Some riders find that the filler cap does not come away instantly. On these machines, to release the filler cap quickly, depress it slightly, then turn it fully anti-clockwise and withdraw the cap. It has two locking positions.

**Use of Petrol Taps.** Many A.M.C. singles have down-draught type Amal carburettors and with such it is important when leaving a machine standing for more than a few minutes always to turn off both the main and reserve-supply petrol taps.

Both taps are of the horizontal-plunger type. As mentioned in a later paragraph, it is advisable normally to run with only the off-side tap open. Refuelling should be undertaken as soon as possible after being forced to draw upon the reserve fuel supply. The reserve supply tap should then be shut immediately. On 1955 and later models, to close either tap, push plunger right in; to open it, pull the plunger right out.

**To Free a Cold Engine.** If the engine (especially a new one) is stone cold, it is generally advisable to free the piston before attempting to start up. Raise the exhaust-valve and kick the engine over smartly about three times.

**Emergency Starting (1958–66 Models).** On the coil-ignition models the ignition switch has an emergency starting position. Should the battery for some reason become badly discharged, turn the ignition switch to the "EMG" position. This connects the alternator direct to the ignition coil and enables the engine to be started independently of the battery. Immediately the engine starts turn the ignition switch to the "IGN" position, otherwise misfiring will develop.

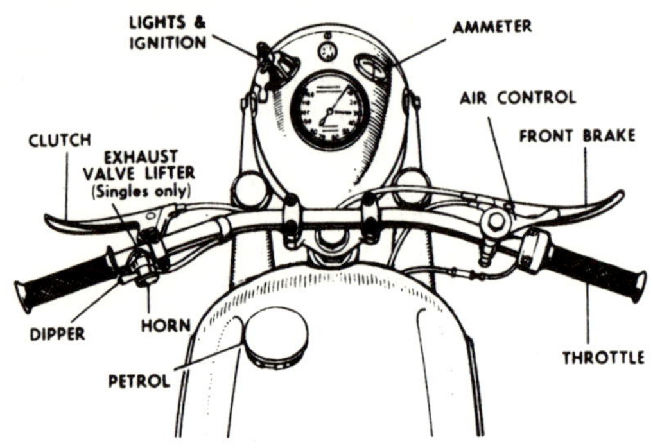


**Fig 1 Layout of handlebar controls**

*All controls are adjustable for angle and are operated by inward movement. Earlier models have a combined dipping switch and horn push and 1958–9 models have an ignition key in the centre of the lighting switch. On more recent models a separate ignition switch is on the off-side of the headlamp.*

**Beware of Excessive Flooding.** Do not adopt the pernicious habit of swamping the carburettor with petrol prior to starting up. Such flooding incurs a grave risk of neat petrol entering the cylinder from a down-draught carburettor and destroying the vital oil film between the piston and cylinder. Dripping petrol also causes a slight fire risk.

**If Engine is Obstinate.** If the engine refuses to start at the third kick, verify that petrol is reaching the float chamber by depressing the tickler. When you are satisfied on this point, remove and carefully inspect the condition of the sparking plug. Clean the plug, check its gap, and refit it (*see* pages 61–64).

**Warm Up Engine Moderately Fast.** Do not race the engine immediately after starting up from cold, as it takes some time for the oil to circulate properly. Too fast running also generates excessive heat. On the other hand, do not warm the engine up too slowly, or the pump will not work fast enough to circulate the oil properly and the combustion of a rather cold mixture will be incomplete, with the result that condensation on and corrosion of the cylinder walls may occur. Never allow the engine to idle for long, especially in hot weather, and do not travel fast until the oil has warmed up.

**Your Speedometer Readings.** The top set of figures on the dial records the total mileage and automatically returns to zero when 100,000 miles is recorded. The bottom set of figures records the mileage since the trip was set to zero, and the red figures indicate tenths of a mile. It is a good plan to set the trip to zero before driving off on each run. To do this, pull and turn to the *right* the knob (protruding from the lower part of the speedometer unit) until "000·0" appears.

## DRIVING HINTS

Ease the machine off its stand, with the engine ticking-over and the foot gear-change pedal in neutral, sit astride the machine, and disengage the clutch, using the handlebar lever (*see* Fig. 1).

**To Engage First Gear.** Raise the foot gear-change pedal *fully* with the toe of the foot and engage first (bottom) gear (*see* Figs. 2–3). Slight backward or forward movement of the machine often facilitates engagement. As soon as the first gear is *felt* to engage, remove the toe from the pedal.

**On a New Machine.** If difficulty is experienced in engaging first gear, wait a few seconds before making another attempt. Initial difficulty in engaging first gear on a *new* machine usually cures itself quite soon, and sticking clutch plates can be rectified by stopping the engine (by raising the exhaust-valve lifter) and smartly operating the kick-starter several times with the clutch fully disengaged.

**Moving Off.** Having engaged first gear, move off by slowly releasing the clutch lever. As the machine gathers speed and the engine takes the full load, gradually increase the throttle opening by means of the twist-grip, so as to maintain a progressive rise in the speed of the engine and machine.

**Changing Up (First to Second).** As soon as your machine has reached a speed of about 15 m.p.h. in first gear, change up into second gear. Once again disengage the clutch, slightly close the throttle, pause a second, and then *depress* the gear-change pedal to its *full extent* with the toe, until second gear is *felt* to engage perfectly. Then engage the clutch and also remove the toe from the pedal to allow the pedal to return to its normal position.

**Changing Up (to Third and Fourth).** Progressively increase the throttle opening until about 20 m.p.h. is obtained. Now disengage the clutch, throttle down slightly, pause a second, and then smartly, but without force, *depress* the gear-change pedal fully until third gear is *felt* to engage perfectly. Engage the clutch, remove the toe from the pedal, and throttle up to maintain a good road speed without any tendency for the engine to "knock." To change into fourth (i.e. top gear) repeat the procedure with the machine travelling quite fast.

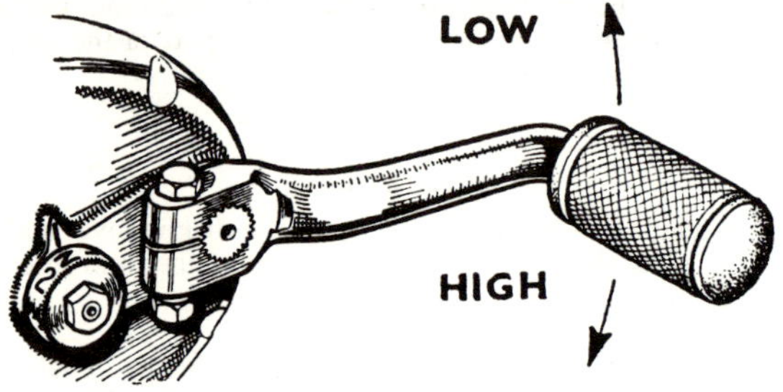


Fig 2 The foot gear-change indicator (1955–6, 1958–66)

*The indicator itself comprises a small drum having the gear positions marked as shown.* N *(neutral) is shown aligned with the dash mark on the gearbox shell.*

**Changing Down (Fourth to Third).** Throttle down to a normal speed for third gear. Disengage the clutch, throttle up slightly, pause a second, and *raise* the gear-change pedal to its *full extent* with the toe of the foot until third gear is *felt* to engage. Immediately afterwards engage the clutch, remove the toe from the pedal, and throttle up to compensate for the increase in the speed of the engine relative to rear wheel speed.

**Changing Down (to Second and First).** The required procedure is similar to that just described for changing down from fourth to third gear. With the toe of the foot *raise* the gear-change pedal to its *full extent* during each gear change. Each full movement of the pedal engages the *next* gear in the gear-change sequence as shown by the indicator in Figs. 2–3.

To change from fourth or third gear into first (bottom) gear, it is not *essential* to complete the full gear-changing procedure for each intermediate gear, although this should be done when hill climbing. The method which can be used is to bring the machine to a crawl by means of the throttle and brakes, disengage the clutch, and then raise the gear-change pedal to its *full extent*—three times or twice (in quick succession), according to whether top or third gear was previously engaged. Each time you raise the gear-change pedal "blip" the engine, i.e. throttle up slightly. Then gently re-engage the clutch.

**Silence is Golden.** Noisy gear changing is bad for sensitive ears, and worse still for the gearbox! Learn to change gear silently. Here are a few golden rules—

1. Make full use of the four gear ratios provided. The gear-change pedal always returns to the same position, but do not forget where it is.
2. Do not "bully" the machine up a steep incline in top gear.
3. Change gear *before* your mount gets "hot and bothered."
4. Use a nicely co-ordinated and almost simultaneous movement when operating the clutch, throttle, and gear-change pedal.
5. Keep a steady pressure on the gear-change pedal and hold the clutch out *until the gear is felt to engage*. At other times remove the foot from the pedal. Never use excessive pressure.
6. Do not race the engine in the lower gears to "impress the lads." They may like it (perhaps), but your engine will hate you!
7. Be kind to the gearbox and give it its oil ration occasionally (*see* page 20).

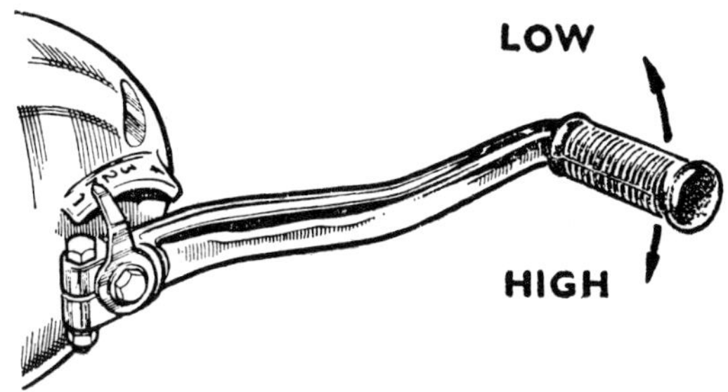


Fig 3 The foot gear-change indicator (1957 Matchless Models)

*The indicator comprises a pointer on the gear-change lever shaft, and a marked quadrant on the gearbox. Norton is similar.*

**Tackling Hills.** Your machine will romp up gentle gradients, but maintain the engine r.p.m. high by making full use of the gearbox where necessary and *in good time*. On no account permit the engine to labour.

Be liberal with the throttle opening, and do not retard the ignition control lever (where fitted) unless this is essential (to ward off a "knock"), as this reduces power output.

When descending steep hills, open the air lever wide and close the throttle. This will not only cool the engine, but it will enable engine compression to exert a powerful braking effect.

**Use Both Brakes.** Acquire the habit of using *both* brakes simultaneously, as this gives powerful braking with minimum and even wear of the brake linings and tyres. It also reduces the tendency for skidding on wet roads.

Excessive and fierce brake application plays havoc with the tyres and transmission, and for this reason you should learn to *drive on the throttle* and use the brakes as little and as seldom as possible. Make use of engine compression as a brake when descending hills (as mentioned above), but never use the clutch, ignition switch (1958–66), or exhaust-valve lifter for controlling speed. This places a motor-cyclist beyond the pale.

Fig 4 To prevent theft use Matchless locking bar and padlock to secure the front forks

*The locking bar is an inexpensive optional extra (Part No. 018691) and can be fitted to most 1955–66 models. Other optional extras include a rear chain case, pannier frames and bags, and crash bar.*

**Bringing Motor-cycle to a Halt.** To effect a normal stop on the road, use the following procedure—

1. Close the throttle by means of the twist-grip.
2. Fully disengage the clutch.
3. Apply *both* brakes simultaneously, increasing the hand and foot pressure as the brakes take effect.
4. Raise the gear-change pedal fully once or several times (according to which gear is already engaged) until you get into first gear. Then depress the pedal *very slightly* with the toe until "neutral" (*see* Figs. 2–3) is obtained.
5. Engage the clutch by gently releasing the lever.

**To Stop the Engine.** After bringing the motor-cycle to a halt with the throttle closed as far as the throttle stop permits (the correct throttle-stop setting is such that when the engine is warmed up and the throttle is closed, the engine ticks-over smoothly, *see* page 30) it is only necessary to raise the exhaust-valve lifter for a few seconds in order to extinguish all signs of life. On 1958–66 models it is not necessary to use the exhaust-valve lifter; just turn the ignition key to the centre. Before you leave your machine, turn off the petrol tap to prevent accidental "flooding."

**Nurse Your Engine for 1000 Miles.** On covering 1000 miles it is not harmful to step up the speed of a *new* machine gradually, but refrain from using full throttle until about 2000 miles have been covered. A new machine must be properly run-in, or it may be permanently spoiled. Here is some sound advice—

1. Don't exceed one-third full throttle for 1000 miles. (For convenience a limit mark can be made on the twist-grip and grip body.)
2. Don't "over-rev." the engine when idling or on the road, especially in the lower gears.
3. Don't exceed 30 m.p.h. in top gear.
4. Don't permit the engine to labour or "knock." Change down in good time and watch the throttle.
5. Don't run the engine with the machine stationary for more than a minute or two.
6. Don't forget to keep the engine, gearbox, and machine correctly lubricated (*see* Chapter 2).

**After the First 400–500 Miles.** A certain amount of bedding-down occurs, and it is important to check the adjustment of the following : (*a*) tappets, (*b*) contact-breaker points, (*c*) steering head bearings, (*d*) primary and secondary chains, and (*e*) brakes. Steering-head bearing adjustment is very important, as slack bearings will suffer. After the initial bedding-down and necessary adjustments have been made, further adjustment is needed much less frequently.

**Avoiding Accidents.** Accidents on the road occur atrociously often. Below is some sound practical advice.

1. Wear a crash helmet. I know (from experience) that a fractured skull and severe concussion can cause a shocking "hangover" for a long period. They can easily be fatal.
2. Do not speed on major roads, or apparently major roads, having minor cross-roads. This can lead to being rammed at right-angles.
3. Exercise special care at cross-roads and roundabouts.
4. Keep a good distance behind car drivers.

5. Always give *clear* hand signals in *ample* time.
6. Do not cut in or indulge in "stunt" riding.
7. Never apply the brakes fiercely on wet roads.
8. Avoid approaching traffic lights too fast.
9. Do not become over-confident and ride excessively fast.
10. Never ride fast in foggy weather.
11. Watch out for pedestrians on pedestrian crossings and crossing the road in front of parked vehicles.

**Ministry of Transport Test Certificate.** A MoT certificate for road worthiness must be obtained from an authorized garage, dealer, or repair shop in respect of any motor-cycle used in the U.K. which was first registered more than *three* years ago. Subsequently this certificate must be renewed *annually*. It must be produced when applying for a registration licence in respect of renewal or change of ownership (Forms V.E.1/A and V.E.1/2 respectively), together with a valid *certificate of insurance* and the current registration book.

The MoT certificate costs 87p and it is legal to ride an untaxed machine to a suitable testing station after making an appointment for a test. The required certificate is issued on the spot if the motor-cycle passes the statutory test for the efficiency of the tyres, brakes, steering, lamps, horn, etc.

# 2 Lubricating Your Model

You would not deliberately ill-treat your machine by running it hard up against a brick wall with the throttle open, but you can be equally cruel to it by neglecting lubrication. This can cause the piston to run hard up against the cylinder walls and cause metal-to-metal contact. The same applies to the numerous bearings.

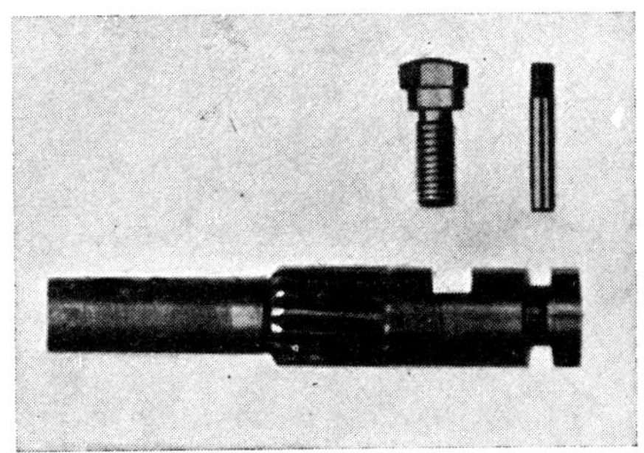

Fig 5 The oil pump plunger, guide screw, and pin

*For position of the pump on engine, see Fig. 6. Note that the hardened steel pin must fit inside the hollow guide screw with the relieved end (shown dark) away from the plunger. The plunger and the guide screw should not be disturbed during routine maintenance. 1964–6 models have a gear-type oil pump (see Fig. 7).*

### THE DRY-SUMP SYSTEM

The engine lubrication system on all these single-cylinder O.H.V. models is of the full dry-sump (D.S.) type, where *all* oil in the engine and oil tank is kept in constant circulation while the engine is running. Its functioning is entirely automatic, but a little regular attention is *essential.*

**The Oil Pump (1955–63 Models).** The pump in the crankcase has a horizontal-type steel plunger (Fig. 5) which combines rotary motion with reciprocating movement. Rotary motion is imparted to the plunger by a

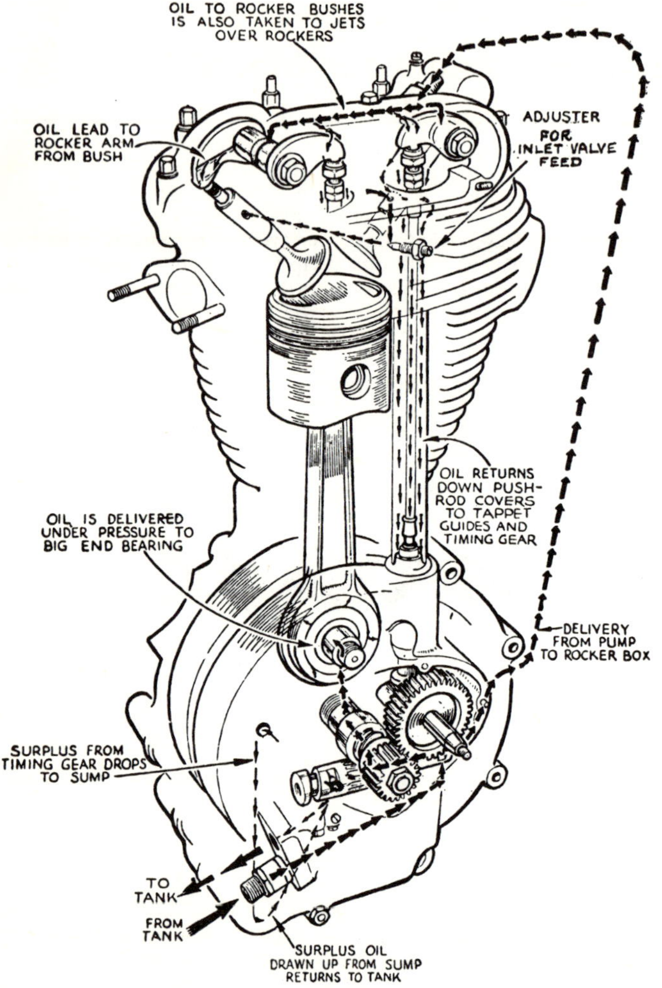


Fig 6 Oil circulation diagram-dry sump (D.S.)

worm on the timing-side engine main-shaft. The reciprocating motion is obtained by the hardened pin in the follow guide screw (*see* Fig. 5) engaging the profiled cam groove cut on the (larger) scavenge end of the plunger.

The profiled cam-groove is designed so that the opening and closing of the two main ports, and a small auxiliary port, are synchronized with the pumping impulses obtained by plunger reciprocation. The scavenge (rear) end of the plunger (which is totally enclosed in its housing by two end-caps) has a greater capacity than the delivery end, and in consequence it keeps the crankcase sump in a "dry" state, all oil being returned to the tank for further circulation.

Fig 7 The "heart" of the 1964–6 lubrication system

*A gear-type oil pump similar to that shown above is used instead of the rotating and reciprocating plunger type shown in Fig. 5. The later pump delivers oil at a higher pressure than the earlier pump.*

**The 1964–6 Oil Pump.** A gear-type oil pump (*see* Fig. 7) is provided on 1964–6 models. The gears on the return side of the pump are twice as wide as those on the feed side and therefore, having twice the pumping capacity, effectively keep the crankcase "dry," all oil being returned to the oil tank for further circulation. The pump, which has no adjustment, is driven by the worm gear on the timing-side mainshaft. Its body is secured by two studs and nuts. A conical shaped heat-resisting rubber oil seal is attached to the pump body where it abuts against a drilling in the timing cover.

**Outline of Oil Circulation.** Fig. 6 shows at a glance how the oil circulates in the A.J.S./Matchless engine with D.S. lubrication. The filtration of the oil in the tank (capacity: 4½ pt, 1955; 5 pt, 1956; 4 pt, 1957–66) is shown in Figs. 8 and 9.

The delivery end of the plunger or gear pump feeds oil under pressure to the timing-side main bearing and connecting-rod big-end bearing through a passage cut in the timing-side main shaft, flywheel, and crankpin. The piston and cylinder bore are lubricated by surplus oil splashed from the big-end bearing. Further provision for lubrication of the cylinder is included on 1955 engines. The oil pump forces oil through a passage (equipped with ball-valve control) in the crankcase to a circular channel in the cylinder base. The oil reaches the cylinder bore through a number of small holes drilled in the channel. Surplus oil automatically drains down into the sump of the crankcase.

The oil pump also feeds a secondary oil-supply to the timing gear and the rocker-box. The supply to the timing gear is fed through a passage in the timing-gear case. The oil collects in the timing-case until a pre-determined level is reached. As may be seen in Fig. 6, on 1955–63 engines an external pipe connected to the front of the oil pump housing conveys the secondary oil-supply direct to the rocker-box and push-rod ends.

The overhead inlet- and exhaust-valve rockers inside the rocker-box are thoroughly lubricated by means of jets above them. In addition, oil is fed to the rocker bushes and (1955 onwards) each rocker arm. The surplus oil drains to and lubricates both valve guides. The oil supply to the guide for the inlet valve can be regulated by means of a needle-pointed screw adjuster. This oil-supply adjustment is the only one provided on the Matchless D.S. lubrication system.

Surplus oil from the valve guides passes down the push-rod covers and the tappet guides and enters the timing-case. Here all engine oil, beyond that needed to keep the level at the pre-determined height, drains down into the sump of the crankcase.

On Norton models 19, ES2 and 50 a by-pass pipe leads from the oil *return* pipe to a banjo union on the rocker-box. Oil is thus fed to the rocker shafts and the ball ends of the overhead rockers. All surplus oil drains down to the crankcase through the two push-rod cover tubes. Surplus from the compartments housing the valve springs drains to the crankcase through holes drilled in the cylinder head and barrel.

**The Oil Tank Filters.** Clean every 5000 miles. A cut-away view of the Matchless oil tank is shown in Figs. 8 and 9. As may be observed, a metal gauze filter is incorporated in the delivery or feed-pipe union. It should be noted that the sole object of this filter is to trap any dirt, pieces of fluff, etc., which may get into the oil tank while it is being replenished.

The main filter (on 1955 models) is a detachable fabric-type. It comprises a long felt element contained within an upright tubular wire cage. As may be noticed in Fig. 8, all the engine oil returned by the scavenge end of the pump has to percolate through the felt element and wire cage which are supported by a cylindrical housing inside the tank. Very thorough filtering results. On 1956–65 models a fabric-type filter with felt element is omitted. Instead, a cylindrical filter of fine metal-gauze is secured in the tank end of the feed-pipe union (*see* Fig. 9).

## LUBRICATING THE ENGINE

Always purchase engine oil in sealed containers or replenish from branded cabinets. Specify clearly the brand and grade which you require, and refuse firmly but politely the "just as good" type.

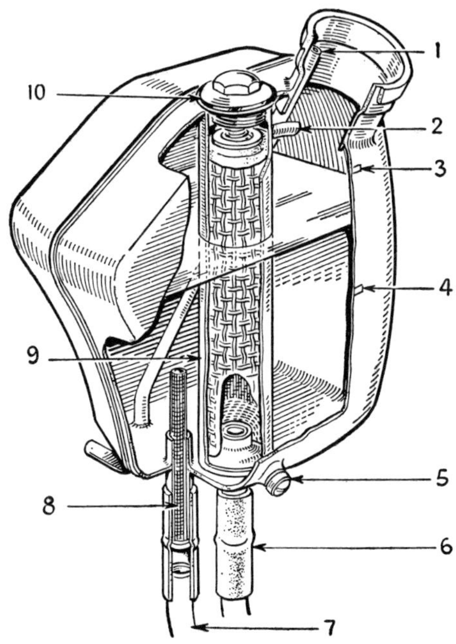


Fig 8 Cut-away view of oil tank showing the filters, etc. (1955)

1. *Vent pipe (to prevent air locks)*
2. *Oil-return pipe orifice*
3. *Top level mark*
4. *Low level mark*
5. *Drain plug*
6. *Oil-return pipe*
7. *Oil-feed pipe*
8. *Gauze filter*
9. *Tube enclosing felt element*
10. *Cap on main filter*

**Suitable Brands and Grades of Engine Oil.** To ensure easy starting, maximum performance and minimum wear, the safest policy is to use one of the brands and grades officially recommended by Norton Villiers Ltd. They recommend the use of one of the following engine oils—

(*a*) Castrol "XXL" (summer) or "XL" (winter).

(*b*) Mobiloil "BB" (summer) or "A" (winter).

(*c*) Shell X-100 40 (summer) or X-100 30 (winter).
(*d*) B.P. Energol SAE 40 (summer) or B.P. Energol SAE 30 (winter).
(*e*) Esso Motor Oil 40/50 (20 W/30 during winter).

It should be noted that the above recommendations are not tabulated in any priority order. It is for the rider to choose which brand he prefers. All the five mentioned are thoroughly sound.

**Checking Level of Oil in Tank.** Remove the filler cap and inspect the level of oil prior to every ride. Always verify the level very carefully before a long run and top-up with suitable engine oil (*see* previous paragraph) if necessary. Sufficient oil must be kept circulating in order to ensure correct lubrication of the engine and its proper cooling.

Never allow the oil level to fall below the low level mark, otherwise the oil in circulation is apt to become hot, dirty, and diluted. As far as possible maintain the oil level at or near the top level mark on the outside of the tank (1955–66), but do not allow the level to rise above this mark. This is important for the following reason.

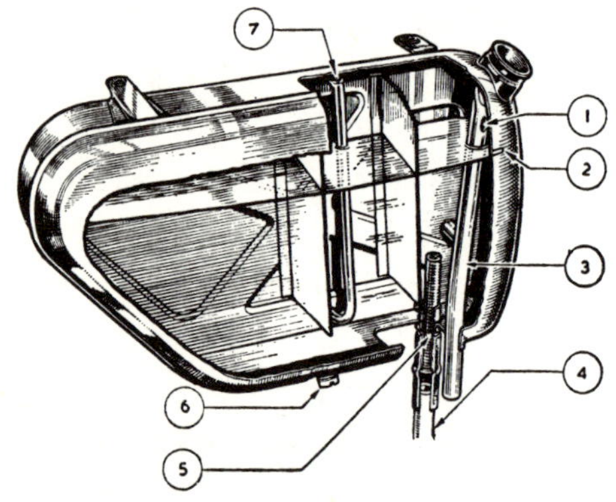


Fig 9 Cut-away view of redesigned oil tank (1956–66 models)

1. *Oil-return pipe orifice*
2. *Top level mark*
3. *Oil-return pipe*
4. *Oil-feed pipe*
5. *Gauze filter (metal)*
6. *Drain plug*
7. *Air vent pipe*

On stopping the engine, no further pump action occurs, but the oil continues to drain into the sump from various parts of the engine. When the engine is subsequently started there is obviously surplus oil accumulated in the sump and this is immediately pumped back into the tank by the large-capacity scavenge side of the oil pump. The effect is to cause an excessive rise in the level of oil in the tank, and possibly oil leakage via the tank air-vent (provided to avoid air locks).

**Verifying Oil Circulation.** Verify the oil circulation before *every run*, immediately after starting up the engine from cold. Remove the oil tank filler-cap and observe the oil flow from the return pipe spout about 2 in. below the filler-cap orifice. If no oil can be seen emerging from return pipe, raise the exhaust-valve lifter and stop the engine immediately.

The oil flow immediately after starting up the engine from cold should be *steady*. An erratic or weak flow is abnormal and requires investigation. After a brief period of warming up the engine, the surplus oil in the crankcase sump is disposed of, and thereafter the oil flow from the spout of the return pipe decreases somewhat and may become irregular. Some froth may be noticeable caused by the presence of air bubbles, but this is normal and can be disregarded, once the engine gets into its stride.

If you suddenly accelerate the engine and then close back the throttle, you may observe first a marked decline, or even cessation, of the oil flow and then a considerable increase in the flow.

**No Oil Pump Adjustment Provided.** The oil pump is capable of delivering the correct volume of oil to the engine at *all* throttle openings. Consequently there is no adjustment provided for the main oil supply. To ensure correct lubrication of the engine, however, it is essential on 1955–63 engines to keep the two end-caps of the plunger housing quite airtight. Check the securing nuts periodically for tightness with a spanner. (*See* also page 18.)

**Adjusting Oil Supply to Inlet Valve Stem.** The adjuster for the oil supply to the inlet valve stem comprises a needle-pointed screw (Fig. 6) situated on the off-side of the cylinder head. If the engine is mechanically sound, the approximately correct setting of the adjuster screw is *one-sixth of a complete turn from the fully closed position*. Once the correct setting has been obtained, it should not be necessary to interfere with the adjustment.

The adjuster screw is secured by a lock-nut, which prevents accidental alteration of the adjustment. To *increase* or decrease the oil supply to the inlet valve stem, the adjuster screw must be turned slightly *anti-clockwise* or clockwise respectively, after first loosening the lock-nut.

What symptoms indicate that an adjustment is called for? An excessive oil supply is denoted by blue smoke at the exhaust, high oil consumption, and a tendency for the sparking plug to oil-up and become dirty. An insufficient oil supply is indicated by the inlet valve stem developing a mouse-like squeak.

**Lubrication of Exhaust Valve Stem.** No adjustment is provided for the oil supply to the exhaust valve stem. The stem is automatically lubricated by oil fed through a channel drilled in the cylinder head. Surplus oil from the exhaust valve stem and from the stem of the inlet valve is by-passed back into the chamber responsible for lubricating the timing gears.

**Changing the Oil.** With a brand-new engine it is advisable to empty the oil tank and replenish it with fresh oil after covering 500 miles and again at 1000 miles. After this, change the oil once every 2000–3000 miles. Also clean the tank filter (two on 1955 models).

Before draining the oil tank, make sure that your machine is level with both wheels on the ground or with the stand down. Then to drain the tank, place a suitable receptacle below the drain plug to catch the oil and unscrew the plug from the off-side edge of the tank. Be patient and allow the whole of the oil to drain.

Having drained the oil tank, also remove the drain plug from the bottom of the crankcase sump (on the off-side), and permit any accumulation of oil to drain off. There will not be a large amount, but it is desirable to remove what there is. A powerful magnetic filter is fitted to the crankcase drain plug on 1956 and later models and its is important to see that the accumulation of any fine metallic particles is completely removed. Finally, make sure that both drain plugs are replaced and firmly tightened.

**The Magnetic Crankcase Filter (1956–66).** *Not fitted to Nortons.* To get access to this filter for cleaning, it is only necessary to unscrew the crankcase drain plug which embodies the magnetic filter.

Forcibly wipe off with a greased rag all metal particles adhering to the magnetic filter (they do this strongly). If you place the filter on the bench, see that the magnet does not come into contact with large iron or steel objects, such as a vice, otherwise some loss of magnetism may occur. Also avoid placing the magnet close to iron or steel filings, which will be attracted to the magnetic filter and need removing.

**Cleaning Tank Filters.** Thorough and regular cleaning of the two filters in the oil tank (one, 1956–66) is important and must never be overlooked. It is best to remove and clean the filter(s) when the engine oil is changed. Advice on removing the filters is given in subsequent paragraphs. As regards actual cleaning, this should be done thoroughly with petrol, but do not attempt to remove the felt element of a large cartridge-type filter from its tubular wire cage, and do not use a fluffy rag when cleaning a metal gauze filter. Allow to dry afterwards.

Inspect the cork washer fitted below the hexagon cap of a fabric filter (Fig. 8) and renew the washer if it is not in perfect condition. Also examine the felt element very carefully. Fit a new element if its ends are at all distorted or perforated.

It should be observed that a choked gauze filter can completely or partially starve the engine of oil, since it is secured to the feed-pipe union and all oil entering the engine has to pass through it.

If the felt element of a fabric filter is clogged up with impurities, excessive lubrication can occur owing to resistance offered to the returning oil causing a "build-up" of oil in the sump. Renew the filter element if its condition is poor.

**To Remove Felt Element (1955 Models).** Unscrew and remove the hexagonal cap from the oil tank filler-orifice. Next withdraw the dished washer and the filter spring. After withdrawing the dished washer and filter spring, insert a finger in the exposed open end of the felt element and gently strain outward and forward to avoid fouling the dualseat. Be most careful not to kink the element when doing this.

The procedure for replacing the filter element is the reverse of that just described.

**To Remove Gauze Filter (1955–66).** Referring to Fig. 9, first drain the oil tank and then (1955–6) free the oil-feed pipe from the rubber connecting-sleeve on the small oil-feed pipe from the base of the tank. If the gauze filter comes away with the rubber connecting-sleeve (1955–6) or feed pipe (1957–66), do not disturb it. If, however, the filter remains in the small pipe attached to the tank, grasp the ringed open end and pull the filter out of the pipe. Replace the filter in the reverse order of removal.

**Note Concerning Oil Pipe Unions.** The unions for the oil tank delivery and return pipes are very close to each other at the crankcase (*see* Fig. 6). When disconnecting an oil pipe be extremely careful not to allow the spanner to foul the union adjacent to the union from which the pipe is being disconnected. Carelessness in this matter can result in a *fractured crankcase.*

**To Remove Oil Pump Plunger (1955–63).** Do not remove the plunger unnecessarily. If you must remove it, first drain the oil tank as described on page 16. Also unscrew the union nut securing the bottom end of the oil-feed pipe from the pump housing to the rocker-box. Remove both end-caps from the pump housing by undoing the hexagon-headed securing bolts.

Just below the pump housing in front of the rear cap is the all-important guide screw and pin. Remove these together (*see* Fig. 5), and push out from the front the pump plunger and withdraw it from the rear end of the pump housing.

**To Replace Oil Pump Plunger.** First make sure that the inside of the pump housing is clean, and also check that the plunger itself is clean internally and externally. Oil the plunger and gently push it into position. Its smaller end must enter the rear of the pump housing, and the guide screw must next be fitted. Before replacing the guide screw, make certain that the steel pin inside the hollow screw is fitted as indicated in Fig. 5, or serious damage may be caused to the teeth of the pump plunger.

After replacing the guide screw, and while slowly tightening it, move the pump plunger backwards and forwards until the end of the guide-screw pin is felt to engage the profiled cam-groove at the rear end of the plunger. When this happens, tighten the guide screw firmly, but on no account tighten (or rotate the engine) before proper engagement is obtained, otherwise stripping of the teeth on the timing-side engine main-shaft end of the teeth on the plunger is liable to take place.

Fit the pump-housing front and rear end-caps and see that airtight joints are obtained. The two paper washers must be in perfect condition. Renew them if they are damaged in the slightest degree. Make certain when fitting the paper washer for the front end-cap that the small oil hole in the cap itself is not obstructed.

**To Prevent Air Leaks at Pump Housing End-caps.** It is advisable to apply some liquid jointing compound to one side of each paper washer. This side must be fitted in contact with the end-cap. To ensure an airtight joint at each end-cap, it is essential to see that its securing bolts are tightened down evenly and firmly. Tightening should always be effected in a diagonal order. Also occasionally check the delivery and return-pipc union nuts for tightness.

**The Gear-type Pump (1964–6 Models).** It should normally be quite unnecessary to disturb the gear-type oil pump as it is of very robust design. If you do dismantle the pump, when assembling it make sure that the end plates do not protrude over the pump body; they should be just below it.

**Magneto Bearings (1955–7 Models).** These are initially packed with grease by the makers during assembly and further greasing should not be necessary for 10,000–15,000 miles. When a general overhaul becomes necessary it is desirable to remove the magneto and return it to Joseph Lucas, Ltd. of Birmingham, 19, or to one of their service depots, for thorough servicing. No grease nipples are fitted, but the contact-breaker requires periodical oiling.

**The Contact-breaker (All 1955–7 Magneto Models).** On 1955–7 models fitted with a Lucas type SR-1 magneto having automatic ignition-control mechanism on the driving side (behind a bulge on the magneto chain-case cover), about every 3000 miles undo the three captive screws and remove the moulded end-cover. Then apply a spot of clean engine oil to the visible end of the contact-breaker pivot pin. About every 6000 miles loosen the nut securing the contact-breaker spring and lift off the contact-breaker lever (*see* Fig. 32). The spring is slotted to facilitate removal. Then smear the pivot pin with a little Mobilgrease No. 2 or a similar grease.

**Cam and Contact-breaker (1958–66 Models).** On the 1958–66 coil-ignition models the Lucas CAIA type contact-breaker and the automatic ignition-advance mechanism are located inside the timing-case main cover. To obtain access to them, remove the two screws retaining the timing-case outer cover, and withdraw the latter.

About every 6000 miles smear the surface of the cam very lightly with some Mobilgrease No. 2. If this is not available, use some clean *winter* grade engine oil (*see* page 13). Also apply a spot of clean engine oil to the contact-breaker pivot. Squeeze a little grease into the felt wick.

Remove the central fixing bolt and inject a small quantity of clean engine oil into the exposed hole. After replacing the fixing bolt and running the engine for a few minutes, centrifugal force will force out the oil over the ignition-advance mechanism.

The contact-breaker chain on 1959–62 coil ignition Nortons is lubricated by oil fed through the inlet cam spindle bush into the chaincase. Any excess oil in the case drains through the breather pipe.

The "Magdyno" chain on 1955–8 models is lubricated by oil passing through the inlet camshaft bush into the "Magdyno" chain case.

**The Magneto Chain (1955–7 Models).** The magneto driving chain (enclosed in a chain case on the off-side of the engine) is not automatically lubricated like the dynamo chain. It is necessary to add some grease about every 2000 miles. Suitable greases are Mobilgrease No 2, Esso Fluid Grease, or Energrease A.O.

Remove the chain-case cover, and apply suitable grease generously to the chain. Also with a thin metal strip work some of the grease well into the automatic ignition-control mechanism.

## LUBRICATING MOTOR-CYCLE PARTS

**The Dynamo Bearings (1955–7 Models).** The armature bearings of the Lucas type E3LM dynamo, as on the magneto, are packed with grease by the makers on assembly and this should suffice for at least 10,000 miles running, or until it is necessary to make a general overhaul when the dynamo should be removed and returned to Joseph Lucas, Ltd., or to a Lucas service depot for thorough cleaning, overhaul, and lubrication.

**The Dynamo Driving Chain (1955–57).** The Lucas dynamo is chain-driven from the engine shaft by a chain which is completely enclosed in the oil-bath chain case containing the primary chain. Therefore, provided the oil-bath chain case is kept properly replenished, no individual attention to the dynamo chain is necessary. The replenishment of the oil-bath is dealt with on page 24.

**Gearbox Lubrication (1955–66).** Norton Villiers, Ltd., advise the use of summer-grade engine oil (*see* page 13) for the four-speed heavyweight gearbox on the 1955–66 models.

Under normal conditions it is sufficient to check the oil level and if necessary top up the gearbox every 1000 miles with summer-grade through the filler-cap orifice on the top edge of the kick-starter case cover. Excessive filling will result in leakage.

Fig 10 When and where to lubricate (1955 onwards)

*The above lubrication chart (showing a 1955 model G3LS) applies to all 1955 and later O.H.V. singles, but note the following: On 1956–66 models a different type oil tank (see Fig. 9) with a single gauze filter is specified. On 1958–66 models with coil ignition no magneto is fitted, and on 1964–5 models "Roadholder" front forks are provided. (For key see opposite.)*

All 1955–6 Burman gearboxes and the 1957–66 Matchless gear-boxes have an oil-level plug (3, Fig. 11) close to the kick-starter spindle; to top-up the gearbox to the maximum permissible level (content: 1 pt), it is only necessary to pour in engine oil through the filler-cap orifice until it begins to trickle from the level-plug hole. On the 1955–6 Burman four-speed gearboxes the filler cap comprises a slotted and threaded circular cap, but on the 1957–66 Matchless gearboxes the filler cap is replaced by a circular cover secured by two small screws. Removal of the circular cover, incidentally, gives access to the clutch thrust-mechanism.

## KEY TO FIG. 10

| Item No. | Description of Item | Lubrication Required | See Page |
|---|---|---|---|
| 1 | *Oil tank* | *Before each run check oil circulation and level. Top-up as required. Every* 1000 *miles change the oil and clean the filter(s). Also drain oil sump and clean filter.* | 14–18 |
| 2 | *Inlet valve stem* | *If necessary, adjust the oil supply.* | 15 |
| 3 | *Contact-breaker (magneto and coil ignition)* | *Every* 6000 *miles smear a little grease on the lever pivot-pin. On* 1958–66 *coil ignition models every* 6000 *miles smear a little grease on the cam and apply a drop of engine oil to the contact-breaker pivot. Squeeze a little grease into the felt wick.* | 19 |
| 4 | *Magneto chain* (1955–7) | *Every* 2000 *miles repack the chain with grease.* | 19 |
| 5 | *Gearbox* | *Every* 1000 *miles top up with summer-grade engine oil to the correct level. Every* 5000 *miles change the lubricant.* | 20 |
| 6 | *Primary chain* | *Every* 500 *miles check level in oil-bath and top-up if necessary to bottom of inspection-cap orifice.* | 22 |
| 7 | *Secondary chain* | *Every* 500 *miles apply grease or engine oil if dry. In wet weather, remove, clean, and grease every* 2000 *miles.* | 23 |
| 8 | *Front and rear hubs* | *Every* 1000 *miles apply the grease gun to the hub nipples. Repack* 1964–6 *hub bearings every* 10,000 *miles.* | 24 |
| 9 | *The brakes* | *Every* 1000 *miles apply the grease gun to the expander-bush nipples. Weekly oil the brake linkage.* | 24 |
| 10 | *Steering head* | *Every* 1000 *miles grease both bearings with the grease gun.* | 24 |
| 11 | *Front-brake cable* | *Weekly oil the exposed end.* | 24 |
| 12 | *Rear-brake pedal* | *Every* 3000 *miles apply the grease gun to the heel nipple.* | 24 |
| 13 | *Speedometer* | *Every* 3000 *miles inject grease through the nipple on top of the speedometer gearbox.* | 24 |
| 14 | *Handlebar levers* | *Weekly apply a little oil to all moving parts. Inject some oil into the cables (where nipples are provided).* | 25 |
| 15 | *Stand* | *Occasionally oil fulcrum bolt.* | 25 |
| 16 | *Front forks* | *Every* 5000 *miles* (1955–63 *models) check the hydraulic fluid content of both "Teledraulic legs," and top up if necessary. On* 1964–6 *models with "Roadholder" forks replenish at* 10,000-*mile intervals each fork leg* (5 *fluid ounces of damping oil).* | 25–27 |
| 17 | *Spring Frame* | *Occasionally grease* 1956–66 *Girling cam-ring adjusters.* | 28 |

**Changing the Gearbox Oil.** After the first 500 miles and thereafter about every 5000 miles change the lubricant in the gearbox. The oil should be drained completely, the A.M.C./Burman gearbox flushed out with a suitable flushing oil and afterwards replenished with $\frac{1}{2}$–1 pt of summer-grade engine oil.

The screwed drain-plug is located low down at the rear of the gearbox shell. Before replenishing the gearbox make sure that the drain plug is replaced and firmly tightened.

**Replenishing Oil-bath Chain Case.** Remove the inspection cap from the oil-bath chain case about every 500 miles and observe the level of oil. On no account must the oil level be permitted to fall below $\frac{3}{16}$ in. from the bottom edge of the inspection-cap orifice, with the machine standing vertically on level ground. The bottom chain run should be just in contact with the oil. The correct amount of oil is present when its surface is just below the bottom edge of the inspection orifice.

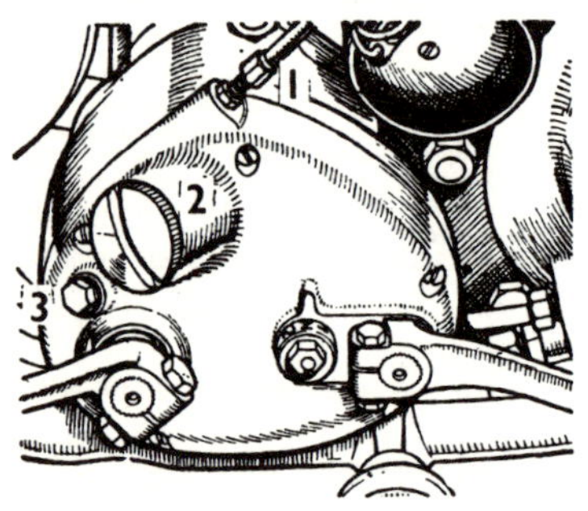


Fig 11 The 1955–6 Burman gearbox

1. *Clutch-cable adjuster.* 2. *Filler cap.* 3. *Oil-level plug.*
*(By courtesy of "Motor Cycle" London)*

If the oil level is too low, some harshness in the primary transmission generally develops, except on 1957–66 models where a sliding oil seal in the form of two steel discs surrounds the gearbox mainshaft. Top-up the oil-bath chain case as required and when necessary, using one of the brands of summer grades of oils mentioned on page 13. Lubrication must not be neglected, for the oil-bath is responsible for lubricating: (*a*) the primary chain, (*b*) the dynamo chain, and (*c*) the engine shaft shock-absorber. Items (*b*) and (*c*) are omitted on 1958–66 models.

**Oil-bath Inspection Cap Removal (1955–57).** To remove the cap, unscrew the knurled screw approximately *four turns*. Then slide the cap sideways until it is possible to slip the back plate through the orifice and remove the complete cap assembly.

To prevent the risk of the filler cap, or inspection cap, being lost while riding, it is important to centralize the cork washer before firmly tightening the knurled retaining screw. Do not forget this when replacing the inspection cap.

**Oil-bath Inspection Cap Removal (1958–66).** On 1958–66 models with an aluminium oil-bath chain case, to remove the inspection cap apply the appropriate spanner (Part No. 018178) to the slot machined in the screwed cap.

**Secondary Chain Lubrication.** About every 500 miles examine the condition of the secondary chain. If the chain is in a dry state, turn the rear wheel by hand and apply some grease or engine oil with a brush or oil-can. About every 2000–3000 miles in wet weather, it is advisable to remove the chain from the sprockets and clean and lubricate in the following manner—

1. Clean the chain thoroughly with paraffin.
2. Hang up the chain and allow to dry.
3. Immerse the chain for at least *ten minutes* in a suitable receptacle containing Mobilgrease No. 2, B.P. Energrease A.O., Esso Fluid Grease, or Castrolease Grease Graphited. The grease should be heated until just fluid and maintained in this state during the period of chain immersion.

Having lubricated the chain, fit it to the gearbox and rear wheel sprockets. It is permissible to lubricate the chain using engine oil instead of one of the greases mentioned but this substitute is not so good. Allow the chain to soak for *at least an hour* where engine oil is used.

**Recommended Greases to Use.** For hub lubrication and the lubrication of all frame parts having grease nipples the following greases are recommended by the makers of all these motor-cycles: Castrolease LM, Mobilgrease MP, Shell Retinax A or C.D., Energrease L2, or Regent Marfax. The grease must, of course, be applied with a grease gun to the Multipurpose 2 nipples provided.

**Filling Grease Gun.** The grease gun (Part No. 017246) provided with the tool kit must be applied periodically to all grease nipples provided on the machine.

Suitable greases to use for various motor-cycle parts are those recommended above. The grease gun must be charged so that the grease is on the *top* side of the piston. Special grease canisters are available with loose collars provided with holes. To charge the grease gun from one of these canisters, place the barrel of the gun over the hole in the central floating plate and press downwards firmly. Turn the grease gun and at the same time remove it from the floating plate. This should charge the grease gun so that the grease is flush with the top of the barrel. Having charged the grease gun, replace its screwed top cap. If no grease canister of the type referred to is available, charge the grease gun by hand, using a suitable lath or similar implement.

**The Wheel Hubs (1955–63 Models).** On new machines the hubs of both wheels are packed with grease. To prevent mud and water entering the hubs, and to ensure correct lubrication, inject some grease by the nipple through the hole in the hub disc of each hub about every 1000 miles. Avoid excessive lubrication, or some of the grease may get on to the brake linings and impair the efficiency of the brakes. 1964–6 hub bearings are packed with grease (*see* below).

**The Wheel Hubs (1964–6 Models).** The hubs have no grease nipples provided. The hub bearings on new machines are packed with sufficient grease for about 10,000 miles. Subsequently about every 10,000 miles remove both wheels (*see* pages 119 onwards), dismantle the hubs, and clean and repack their bearings with fresh grease.

**The Steering Head.** Apply the grease gun sparingly to the grease nipple in the head lug of the frame about every 2000 miles. Also grease the nipple (where fitted) on the right-hand side of the handlebar lug at the same time.

**Lubricating Front and Rear Brakes.** Inject a little grease about every 1000 miles through the grease nipple provided on each brake cover-plate for the expander bush. About every 3000 miles apply the grease gun to the nipple of the rear-brake pedal.

Smear a few drops of engine oil *weekly* on the yoke-end pins at the front and rear ends of the rear-brake rod. Do not forget the threaded portion of the rod to which the hand adjuster is fitted. Also remember the exposed end of the front-brake cable.

**Speedometer Lubrication.** To ensure smooth and efficient running, grease the speedometer gearbox every 3000 miles. The gearbox is attached to the rear-wheel spindle on the off-side and the grease nipple is located on top of the speedometer gearbox. No further lubrication is required beyond the above-mentioned attention.

**Lubricating Throttle Twist-grip.** Stiffness sometimes develops and this spoils sensitive control of the throttle. To rectify stiffness is quite simple, and the following procedure should be adopted.

1. Remove both the screws which retain the halves of the twist-grip clip.
2. Withdraw the twist-grip from the end of the handlebars.
3. Smear some grease on the off-side part of the handlebars over which the twist-grip fits.
4. Smear some grease on the friction spring, and also on the drum on which the internal wire is wound.
5. Replace the twist-grip on the end of the handlebars.
6. Fit the two screws retaining the halves of the twist-grip clip and firmly tighten the screws.

**The Handlebar Levers.** It is advisable to apply a little engine oil *weekly* to all the moving parts of the handlebar levers. This will reduce friction and keep the controls responsive and easy to operate.

On most 1955–7 models the control cables for the throttle slide and the clutch lever have a grease nipple. Some engine oil should be injected at the first indication of jerky or stiff action. When using the gun, hold it as nearly vertically as possible, with the nozzle facing *downward.*

**The Dipper Switch.** Every 5000 miles lubricate the moving parts of the dipper switch with a little thin machine oil.

**Lubricating Stand Fulcrum Bolts.** Occasionally lubricate the stand fulcrum bolts; apply some engine oil with an oil-can. There are several small parts on the machine where only a little movement occurs. All such parts should be similarly lubricated. This will facilitate free movement and prevent rusting. The main parts of the machine requiring attention are indicated in the lubrication chart on page 20.

**If a Sidecar is Fitted.** Do not forget to lubricate the sidecar chassis. Several grease nipples are provided for the purpose.

**Hydraulic Fluids for "Teledraulic" Front Forks (1955–63).** The "Teledraulic" front forks require no actual lubrication. It is necessary, however, occasionally to check the hydraulic fluid content of each fork leg (6½ fluid ounces); top-up if necessary, as described in later paragraphs of this chapter. Below are specified suitable types of fluid for the hydraulic dampers—

1. Wakefield's "Castrolite" (SAE-20).
2. Mobiloil "Arctic" (SAE-20).
3. Shell X-100 Motor Oil 20/20W (SAE-20).
4. B.P. Energol (SAE-20).
5. Essolube "20" (SAE-20).

**To Check Hydraulic Fluid Content (1955–63 "Teledraulics").** It is wise every 5000 miles to check the hydraulic-fluid content of each front-fork leg. Before beginning this check, it is necessary to see that your machine is quite vertical, with the weight on both wheels. Place a suitable box beneath each footrest. Remove the two hexagon-headed plugs from the tops of the fork leg inner tubes, after levering off (1955) the snap-on dome caps, or removing the rubber grommets (1956–63).

To determine the fluid content of each fork leg, remove the drain plug from the base of the fork-leg slider and permit the hydraulic fluid to drain off into a graduated measuring jug or other vessel having a capacity of at least 10 fluid ounces. Most of the fluid will drain off, but not all of it will do so.

Replace the drain plug in the base of the fork-leg slider on 1955–7 models. On these models the damper rod is attached to the hexagon-headed plug at the top of each fork leg and it is necessary to work each damper rod up and down, employing a pumping action. Hold the top plug with the fingers only, and make very sharp *upward* strokes. Wait two minutes and then remove the drain plug a second time and catch any further hydraulic fluid which may drain off into the graduated vessel already containing most of the fluid.

It may be necessary to repeat the 1955–7 procedure (that is working the forks or top plugs up and down) several times to ensure that the maximum quantity of hydraulic fluid is drained off into the graduated vessel. Note the total amount of fluid extracted. It is not possible to extract by draining the whole content of each leg (6½ fluid ounces), but the amount drained off and measured should total 6 fluid ounces.

**Topping-up Procedure (1955–63 "Teledraulics").** The checking of the hydraulic-fluid content and the topping-up of each fork leg should be effected in one continuous operation. Deal with each fork leg individually. It is assumed that the fluid content of the leg has already been determined. Then top-up as follows—

1. If the total amount of hydraulic fluid extracted from the fork leg measures exactly 6 fluid ounces, no topping-up is necessary. If the amount is less than the appropriate quantity just stated, add hydraulic fluid (of the type already in use) to the graduated vessel until the total amount of fluid measures exactly 6 fluid ounces.
2. Replace the drain plug in the base of the fork slider.
3. Pour the 6 fluid ounces contained in the graduated vessel into the top of the fork inner-tube.
4. Replace the hexagon-headed top plug (and rubber washer), and firmly tighten the plug. Also replace the snap-on dome cap (1955) or rubber grommet (1956–63).

It is important to note that where 1955–63 "Teledraulic" front forks have been completely stripped down (necessarily incurring the removal of *all* hydraulic fluid), it is essential after assembly to top-up each fork leg with

6½ fluid ounces, not the quantity (½ fluid ounce less) just quoted for topping-up.

**Replenishing 1964–6 "Roadholder" Front Forks.** These telescopic front forks are of entirely different design to the 1955–63 "Teledraulic" forks, but the same type of damping oils referred to on page 25 are suitable. The normal oil content is 5 fluid ounces (142 c.c.). The damping oil should be drained and replenished after the first 1000 miles and subsequently at 10,000-mile intervals or whenever the forks appear to have deteriorated.

The fork springs abut against the filler plugs and therefore before removing these plugs it is essential to take the weight off the front wheel by placing the machine on its central stand. Otherwise the forks are likely to collapse. With the machine on its central stand unscrew the two top hexagon-headed filler plugs. Now place a suitable receptacle to catch oil draining off from the fork leg first to be dealt with. Remove the drain plug screw. This is the small screw on the rear side at the bottom of the fork leg. Be careful not to lose the small washer for the drain plug. Allow all oil to drain off. Draining is assisted by tilting the wheel to one side. Drain the other fork leg in a similar manner. Finally replenish both fork legs after replacing both drain plugs and their washers. See that the drain plugs are firmly tightened. Use a measured container to pour 5 fluid ounces of damping oil into the top of each fork leg. Afterwards replace the two filler plugs and their washers. Note that the air-space between the fork springs and the insides of the tubes is very small and replenishment must be done with extreme care to avoid loss of oil by spilling.

**"Teledraulic" Rear-suspension Units (1955–6).** The rear-suspension units have hydraulic damping springs of almost identical design to that used for the "Teledraulic" front forks. But only if leakage of hydraulic fluid occurs (most unlikely) is it necessary to replenish the fork legs with the correct amount of fluid. Should the leg action become excessively lively, it is possible that some loss of damping fluid is responsible.

The correct fluids to use are those specified on page 25. Each fork leg should contain exactly 85 c.c. or a little below 3 fluid ounces. On no account must the oil content exceed 90 c.c.

**Girling Rear-suspension Units (1957–66).** These proprietary units are sealed by the makers and do not require to be topped-up. During initial assembly their springs are lubricated and sufficient hydraulic fluid inserted in the damper units.

Occasionally clean and grease the cam-rings adjusters provided to give three different spring tensions. If the movement of the telescopic legs is accompanied by a rubbing noise or squeaking, remove the two half circlips securing each top cover-tube, remove the tube, and apply some grease to the outside of the spring.

**The "Swinging Arm" (1955–66).** The "swinging arm" assembly in whose rear end the rear wheel is mounted is hinged just behind the gearbox, and the "swinging arm" fork-hinge plain bearings are automatically lubricated from a reservoir containing 1½ fluid ounces (42.6 c.c.) of heavy gear oil. This should suffice to lubricate the bearings for an almost indefinite period. Slight oil leakage may occur on a new machine (or where the reservoir has been replenished), but this is of no significance and stops after a few hundred miles have been covered. If replenishment should ever become necessary, remove the small screw from the off-side hinge bearing-cap and top-up the oil reservoir with heavy gear oil (SAE-140) to the level of the screw orifice.

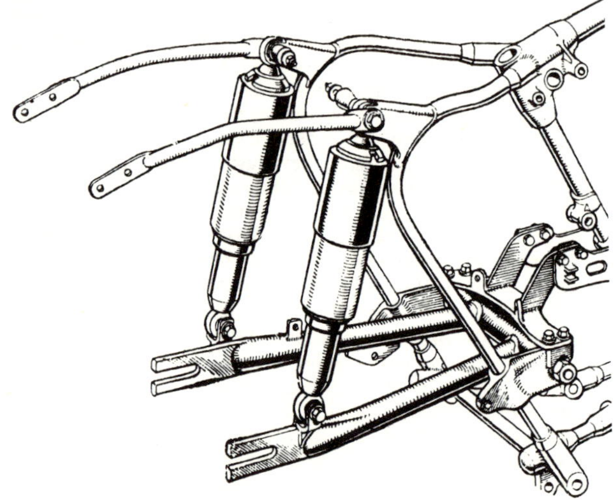

Fig 12 Norton "swinging arm" rear suspension and shock-absorbers (1955–8)

*(By courtesy of "Motor Cycle" London)*

# 3 Correct Carburation

All 1955–66 single-cylinder 350 c.c. and 500 c.c. engines have a "Monobloc" type Amal needle-jet carburettor fitted.

## "MONOBLOC" AMAL CARBURETTOR

The Amal "Monobloc" carburettor specified on all 1955 and later O.H.V. singles differs from the standard type, used prior to 1955, in several respects. But its general functioning is similar. The "Monobloc" design includes: a horizontal float chamber made integral with the carburettor body; a float needle of moulded nylon; a top petrol feed; a needle jet with bleed holes giving two-way compensation; and a detachable pilot jet which can be easily cleaned.

Fig. 13 shows all the essential parts of the instrument. The float chamber (13) and needle (9) maintain a constant level of petrol in the needle jet (14) and the pilot jet (17). The selection by the makers of the appropriate jet sizes and main-bore choke ensures a proper atomizing and proportioning of the petrol and air sucked into the engine.

The air valve (3) is normally kept fully raised, and the throttle valve (24) controlled by the handlebar twist-grip controls the volume of mixture, and therefore the power. At all throttle openings a correct mixture is automatically obtained.

The "Monobloc" carburettor, like the standard instrument, operates in four stages. When opening the throttle from the fully closed position to one-eighth open (for tick-over) the mixture is supplied by the pilot jet (17), and the strength of the mixture is determined by the setting of the knurled pilot air-adjusting screw (20) which has a coil locking spring to facilitate ajustment. As the throttle is opened slightly farther, the main jet system comes into action, the mixture being augmented by the main jet (16) through the pilot by-pass.

The amount of cut-away on the atmospheric side of the throttle valve regulates the petrol-to-air ratio between one-eighth and one-quarter throttle. The needle jet (14) and the jet needle (23) take over the mixture regulation between one-quarter and three-quarter throttle, and the mixture strength is determined by the relative position of the needle in the clip (4) attached to the throttle valve (24). When the throttle is opened beyond three-quarters, the mixture strength is determined only by the size of the main jet. Note that the main jet (16) does not spray petrol direct into the carburettor mixing-chamber, but discharges through the needle jet into the primary air chamber. From there it enters the main choke through the primary air choke. The latter has a two-way compensating action in conjunction with the "bleed" holes in the needle jet. Pilot and main jet behaviour are not affected by this two-way compensation which governs only acceleration at normal cruising speed.

## TUNING AMAL "MONOBLOC" CARBURETTOR

Normally *it is unwise to interfere with the maker's carburettor setting* (*see* Tables I–IV) unless there is a very special reason for doing so. However, it is sometimes desirable to make a slow-running adjustment with the pilot air-adjusting screw and throttle-stop screw.

To vary the strength of the running mixture, it is necessary to adjust the height of the needle in the throttle valve, or else to fit a larger or smaller size main jet. The condition of the sparking plug provides an excellent guide to the condition of the mixture. The plug body should be black, with no sooty deposits.

**Pilot Jet Adjustment.** This should be effected with the engine already warmed up. If the adjustment is appreciably at fault, screw home the pilot air-adjusting screw fully and then unscrew it (usually about two complete turns) until the engine idles at an excessive speed, with the throttle twist-grip closed and the throttle slide abutting the throttle-stop screw. The air lever should be fully open and the ignition lever (where automatic ignition-advance is not provided) should be set to obtain the best slow-running (half to two-thirds advanced).

Unscrew the throttle-stop screw until the engine slows up and begins to falter. Then screw the pilot air-adjusting screw in or out as required to

---

**KEY TO FIG. 13**

1. *Mixing-chamber cap*
2. *Mixing-chamber lock ring*
3. *Air valve*
4. *Jet-needle clip*
5. *Jet block*
6. *Air passage to pilot jet*
7. *Tickler assembly*
8. *Banjo securing-bolt*
9. *Float needle*
10. *Float*
11. *Float-chamber cover screws*
12. *Float-chamber cover*
13. *Float chamber*
14. *Needle jet*
15. *Main-jet holder*
16. *Main jet*
17. *Pilot jet*
18. *Throttle-stop adjusting screw*
19. *Jet block locating screw*
20. *Pilot air-adjusting screw*
21. *Mixing chamber*
22. *Fibre seal*
23. *Jet needle*
24. *Throttle valve*
25. *Throttle return-spring*

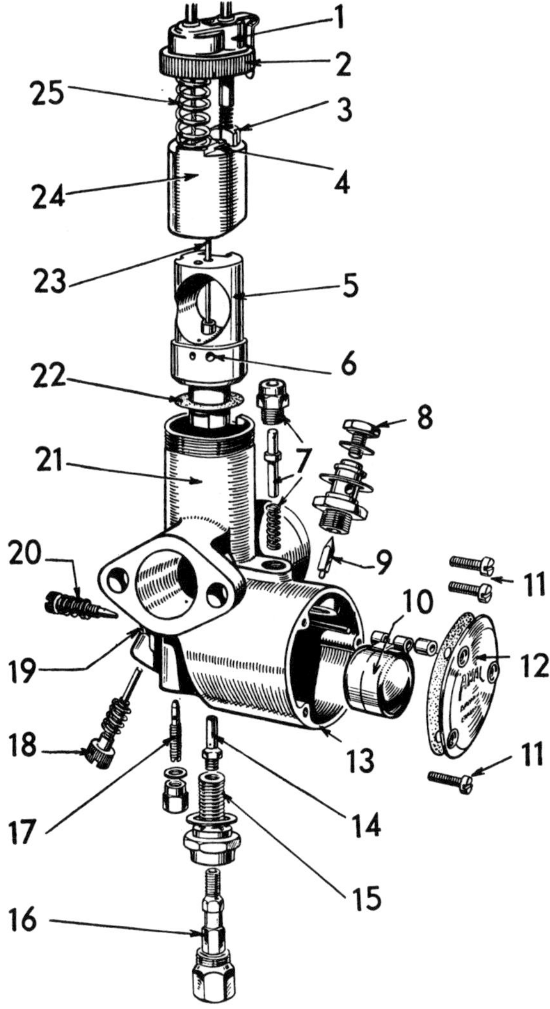


Fig 13 "Monobloc" Amal carburettor (1955 onwards) shown dismantled
*(By courtesy of B.S.A. Motor Cycles Ltd.)*

enable the engine to run regularly and faster. To weaken the mixture, screw the pilot air-adjusting screw *outwards*.

Slowly lower the throttle-stop screw until the engine again commences to falter. Then reset the pilot air-adjusting screw to obtain the best slow-running. If after making this second adjustment the engine ticks over too fast, repeat the adjustment a third time. The combined adjustment sounds complicated but in practice is quite simple. It is important to avoid excessive richness of the slow-running mixture, especially if much riding is done on small throttle openings; if the mixture is too rich, considerable running on the pilot jet will occur while riding, with consequently a high fuel consumption.

Aim at obtaining the best tick-over on a mixture bordering on the weak side. The engine should be on the point of spitting-back.

Rev the engine up and down sharply several times (while at rest and while riding) and note whether the exhaust is nice and crisp, with no "flat spots" as the twist-grip is turned. It is essential to combine good tick-over with good acceleration.

**Pilot Jet Obstruction.** If the adjustment of the pilot jet does not obtain the desired results and the engine will not idle nicely with the throttle almost closed, the air lever fully open, and the ignition lever (where fitted) half to two-thirds advanced, it is possible that the pilot jet is obstructed. The jet passage is very small and can readily become choked.

With the "Monobloc" carburettor (*see* Fig. 13), to remove the pilot jet (17), remove the pilot jet cover-nut and then unscrew the jet itself which should be thoroughly cleaned in petrol and then blown through. See that the air passage (6) to the pilot jet, and also the pilot outlet, are quite clear.

**If Slow-running is Bad.** If it is found impossible to obtain good slow-running by making the pilot jet adjustment as described on page 30, it is probable that some defect other than carburation is responsible for preventing the engine running smoothly at low revolutions. Air leaks or badly-seating valves may weaken the mixture. Defects in the ignition system may also be responsible for poor tick-over. The sparking plug may be oily, or the points set too close (*see* page 62). Possibly the spark is excessively advanced or the contact-breaker needs attention (*see* page 64). Also examine the h.t. cable for signs of shorting, and check the tappet adjustment.

**If Consumption of Fuel is Excessive.** If in spite of careful checking of the tuning of the carburettor, high fuel consumption continues, it is likely that one or more of the under-mentioned causes is responsible for wastage of precious fuel. Late ignition timing will eat into your petrol supplies quickly. The same applies to poor engine compression due to badly-fitting piston rings or valves. Also take into consideration the question of flooding due to a faulty float, air leakage at the joint between the carburettor and engine, weak valve springs. See that no wastage is caused by slack petrol pipe union nuts or leakage from the float-chamber cover.

**Adjusting/Setting Twist-grip.** Adjustment should be such that the grip is free and easy to twist, but "stays put." The spring tension on the twist-grip rotating sleeve is regulated by a screw incorporated in one-half of the twist-grip body. To increase the tension, loosen the lock-nut and tighten the screw in the body as required.

It is possible to move the complete twist-grip on the handlebars by slackening the two screws which clamp it in position. The best position of the twist-grip is that which gives the cleanest and straightest path to the throttle cable between the handlebars and the under side of the petrol tank.

On most 1955–7 models a nipple is provided for lubricating the throttle cable, and so ensure smooth throttle operation. If any stiffness or jerkiness occurs, inject a little engine oil through the nipple. When doing this, apply the gun as nearly vertically as possible with the nozzle downwards.

## MAINTENANCE OF AMAL CARBURETTOR

To ensure correct carburation it is advisable occasionally to remove the carburettor from the engine, strip it down completely, and then thoroughly clean it. It is a good plan to do this about every six months as described below.

**Stripping "Monobloc" Carburettor.** Close both petrol taps and disconnect the twin petrol pipes by undoing the banjo bolt (8) over the float chamber (*see* Fig. 13). Referring to Fig. 13, unscrew the mixing-chamber knurled lock-ring (2) on top of the carburettor and also remove the two nuts securing the carburettor flange to the face of the inlet port. Then remove the body of the carburettor (21), complete with the integral float chamber (13). While removing the carburettor, pull the air valve (3) and the throttle valve (24) from the mixing chamber and tie them up temporarily out of the way. It is rarely necessary to disconnect the slides from the cables. Check that the flange washer is sound.

Further dismantling is straightforward. Referring to Fig. 13, to remove the jet needle (23), withdraw the jet-needle clip (4) on top of the throttle valve, and remove the needle. To obtain access to the float (10), remove the three screws (11) securing the float-chamber cover (12). Lift out the hinged float (10) and withdraw the moulded-nylon needle (9). Lay both aside for cleaning. The float-chamber vent, by the way, is embodied in the tickler assembly (7), and the top-feed union houses a filter element of fine gauze which is readily accessible for cleaning.

**TABLE I**

**CARBURETTOR SETTINGS FOR 1955–6 A.J.S./MATCHLESS SINGLES**

| Model | Car-burettor | Main Jet | Pilot Jet | Throttle Valve | Needle Position |
|---|---|---|---|---|---|
| 350 c.c. (*no* air filter) | 376/5 | 210 | 30 | 376/3½ | 3 |
| 500 c.c. (with air filter) | 376/33 | 200 | 30 | 376/3½ | 3 |
| 500 c.c. (to engine 27000) | 376/14 | 240 | 30 | 376/3 | 3 |
| 500 c.c. (after No. 27000) | 389/1 | 260 | 30 | 389/3½ | 3 |

**TABLE II**

**CARBURETTOR SETTINGS FOR 1957–61 A.J.S./MATCHLESS SINGLES**

| Model (No air filter) | Car-burettor | Main Jet | Pilot Jet | Throttle Valve | Needle Position |
|---|---|---|---|---|---|
| 350 c.c. | 376/5 | 210* | 30 | 376/3½ | 3 |
| 500 c.c. | 389/1 | 260* | 30 | 389/3½ | 3 |

* Reduce by 10 with air filter.

**TABLE III**

**CARBURETTOR SETTINGS FOR NORTON SINGLES 1955–62**

| Model | Main Jet | Pilot Jet | Throttle Valve | Needle Position |
|---|---|---|---|---|
| ES2 (1955–8) | 270 | 30 | 376/4 | 3 |
| ES2 (1955–9) | 270 | 30 | 3 | 3 |
| ES2 (1960–2) | 270 | 30 | 4 | 3 |
| 19 (1955–8) | 270 | 30 | 376/4 | 3 |
| 50 (1955–62) | 270 | 30 | 376/3½ | 2 |

**TABLE IV**

**CARBURETTOR SETTINGS FOR 1962–6 SINGLES**

| Model | Main Jet | Pilot Jet | Throttle Valve | Needle Position |
|---|---|---|---|---|
| 350 c.c. (1962–3) | 230 | 25 | 3½ | 3 |
| 500 c.c. (1962–3) | 300 | 25 | 3½ | 3 |
| 350 c.c. (1964–5) | 260 | 25 | 3 | 3 |
| 500 c.c. (1964–5) | 290 | 25 | 3½ | 3 |

To remove the main jet (16), remove the main-jet cover and unscrew the jet from the jet holder (15), which should also be unscrewed. Remove the jet-block locating screw (19) to the left of and slightly below the pilot air-adjusting screw. Then push or tap out the jet block (5) and fibre seal (22) through the large end of the mixing chamber (21). To remove the pilot jet (17), remove the pilot-jet cover nut and unscrew the jet.

**Cleaning the Carburettor.** Wash all the carburettor components thoroughly clean with petrol and blow through the various ducts and passages to make sure that they are quite clear. Avoid using a fluffy rag for drying purposes. Pay special attention to the small pilot-jet passages in the jet block. See that all impurities are removed from inside the float chamber. On the "Monobloc" carburettor do not forget to clean the detachable pilot jet and the nylon filter inside the banjo for the petrol pipe unions.

**Inspection of Parts.** When dismantling the carburettor it is advisable to make a close inspection of the various parts if the carburettor has been in continuous service for a considerable period.

1. *The Float Chamber*. Examine the components very carefully and check that the vent is unobstructed. The float must be in perfect condition. Clean the moulded-nylon needle on the "Monobloc" carburettor very thoroughly, and be careful not to damage it.
2. *The Throttle Valve*. Test this for fit in the mixing chamber. Should excessive play exist, renew the slide forthwith. See that the new slide has the correct amount of cut-away.
3. *The Jet-needle Clip*. The spring clip securing the tapered needle to the throttle valve must grip the needle firmly, and free rotation must *not* occur, as this causes the needle groove to wear. Always be careful to replace the needle with the lip in the central groove.
4. *The Jet Block*. Before tapping this home in the mixing chamber verify by blowing that the pilot-jet ducts are clear and that the jet-block fibre seal is in good condition.
5. *The Carburettor Flange*. Examine this for truth with a straight-edge. Distortion sometimes occurs, and this may cause an air leak. If the flange face is slightly concave, file and rub down the face with emery cloth laid on a surface plate until it is dead flat and smooth.

If a rubber "O" ring is fitted, replace it if worn.

**Jet Needle Wear.** The needle itself does *not* wear, though some wear of the groove may occur if the jet-needle clip is not grasping the needle firmly. If the mixture is too rich with the clip in No. 1 groove (nearest top end), it is probable that the needle jet needs to be renewed because of wear. It is assumed that the carburettor is correctly tuned and that no flooding occurs (*see* pages 32–33).

**Assembling "Monobloc" Carburettor.** Do this in the reverse order of dismantling. Refering to Fig. 13 screw home the pilot jet (17) and the pilot jet cover-nut, not omitting to replace its washer. Push or tap home the jet block (5) and fibre seal (22) through the large end of the mixing chamber (21). Check that the fibre seal fitted to the stub of the jet block is in good condition. Then fit the jet block locating screw (19). Screw the main-jet holder (15) into the jet block, after checking that the washer for the holder is sound. Next screw the main jet (16) into the jet holder.

Replace the moulded-nylon needle (9) in the float chamber (13), and fit the hinged float (10) with the *narrow* side of the hinge uppermost. Afterwards fit the float-chamber cover (12) and secure by means of the three screws (11). Verify that the cover and body faces are undamaged and quite clean. Renew the washer.

If previously removed, attach the jet needle (23) to the throttle valve (24) and secure with the jet-needle clip (4), making sure that the clip enters the central groove.

Position the carburettor-flange washer, and offer up the carburettor to the face of the inlet port after easing the air and throttle valves (3) and (24) down into the mixing chamber; correctly locate the throttle valve by slight rotation. When easing the throttle valve home, make sure that the tapered jet needle (23) really enters the hole in the jet block (5). Secure the carburettor flange firmly to the engine by means of the two nuts, and tighten these evenly. Tighten down firmly the mixing-chamber knurled cap ring (2) and see that the throttle slide works freely when this is tightened down.

Finally reconnect the twin petrol pipes by tightening the banjo bolt (8) over the float chamber (13).

## THE AIR FILTER

**Maintenance.** An air filter of the "oil-wetted" type is fitted as an optional extra to all these models. In the United Kingdom the roads are excellent and the air comparatively free from dust, and it is questionable whether the fitting of an air filter, except for use abroad in countries where the roads are poor and dusty, will appreciably prolong the life of the cylinder and piston.

Where an air filter is fitted, it is advisable about every 3000 miles to withdraw the filter element; wash it thoroughly in petrol, paraffin, or other suitable solvent, and allow to dry. Then submerge the element completely for a few minutes in thin oil (SAE 20) of the type recommended on page 25 for the "Teledraulic" front forks. Remove the element, allow all surplus oil to drain off, and afterwards replace in the air-filter case. It is desirable to renew the filter element about every 10,000 miles.

**To Remove Filter Element (1956–60 Models.)** Pull the rubber hose off the air-intake of the "Monobloc" carburettor after releasing the clip (1957). Next remove the frame cover and pull off the hose end from the air filter. Then remove the bolts which secure the air filter to the oil tank and frame and remove the complete filter assembly. Note that the filter element is secured in its cage by bolts, nuts, and locking washers.

After cleaning the filter (*see* previous paragraph) replace it. When replacing the hose on the filter, see that it is properly located. The end of the rubber hose is split along the edge of the lip, and it is important to make sure that the neck of the filter assembly enters this groove.

**To Remove Filter Element (1961–6 Models).** First remove the top pivot bolt. Also remove the bottom nut on the filter. Then remove the filter with hose. The filter compartment can now be separated to gain access to the filter element. Maintenance should be effected as described in a previous paragraph.

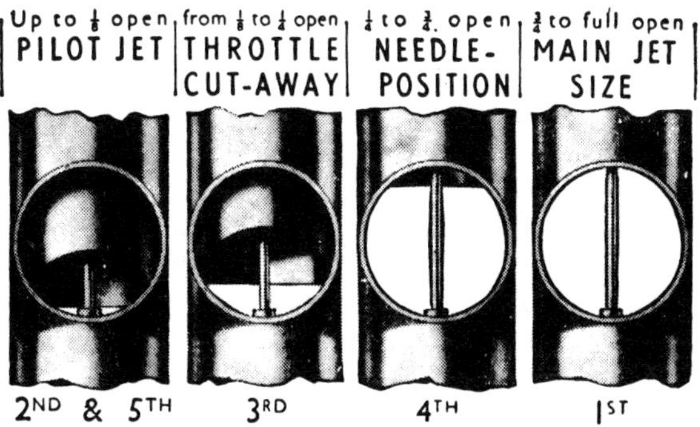


Fig 14 Range and sequence of tuning—Amal carburettor

# 4 Electrical Equipment

To obtain full illumination from the lamps at all times, a little attention to the equipment is normally necessary and in practice is generally confined to: keeping the lamps clean; renewing dud bulbs; topping-up the battery regularly; taking occasional specific gravity readings; periodically inspecting the dynamo brushes and commutator (particularly important on 1955–7 models, but not applicable to any 1958–66 models); the keeping of all connections clean and tight; and the prevention or repair of frayed leads by taping where necessary.

Before making electrical adjustments, always disconnect the positive wire from the battery.

**Lighting Switch Positions.** The lighting switch (*see* Fig. 1) situated on top of 1955–66 headlamps causes the dynamo to charge in all three switch positions, which are as follows—

"OFF"—No lights on.

"L"—Headlamp pilot, rear, and speedometer lights, on.

"H"—Headlamp main, rear, and speedometer lights, on.

**Headlamp Alignment.** Incorrect headlamp alignment gives reduced road illumination and liability to dazzle other road users.

Many garages have a Lucas "Beamsetter," and advantage can be taken of one of these devices. To adjust the headlamp yourself, place your motorcycle so that it faces a light-coloured wall at a distance of about 25 feet. Switch on the main driving light and take vertical measurements from the centre of the headlamp and from the centre of the illuminated circle on the wall to the ground. Both measurements should be the same. If not, loosen the two fixing bolts securing the headlamp body and tilt the headlamp until the centre of the beam is truly parallel with the ground. Then retighten the two fixing bolts securely.

**The 1955–7 Lucas Headlamps.** As may be seen in Fig. 15, two smart torpedo-shaped pilot lamps are secured to the front-fork lamp supports by tubular bolts, through each of which a lead passes to the adjacent pilot lamp. The ammeter and lighting switch are mounted on a panel on top of the headlamp, as shown in Fig. 15 or (on earlier models) as shown in Fig. 25.

On all 1955–7 headlamps, to obtain access to the double filament "pre-focus" main bulb, remove the lamp front (with light-unit assembly) as follows. Loosen the screw on top of the headlamp body, withdraw the rim outward from the top, and as the lamp front emerges raise it a little to free the lower tag from the shell of the headlamp. To get at the bulb in each streamlined pilot lamp, remove the screw at the rear and gently pull forward on the glass rim.

**The 1958–66 Lucas Headlamp.** Details of the Lucas type of headlamp fitted to 1958–66 A.M.C. machines are shown in Fig. 16. The light-unit assembly is shown removed from the headlamp body. On top of the head-lamp body are mounted, as shown in Fig. 15, the Smith speedometer, the ammeter and the lighting switch. The three lighting switch positions are as described on page 38. On 1958–59 models with an alternator and rectifier instead of a dynamo and a magneto, there is an ignition key in the centre of the lighting switch; a separate ignition switch is provided on the off-side on 1960–6 models.

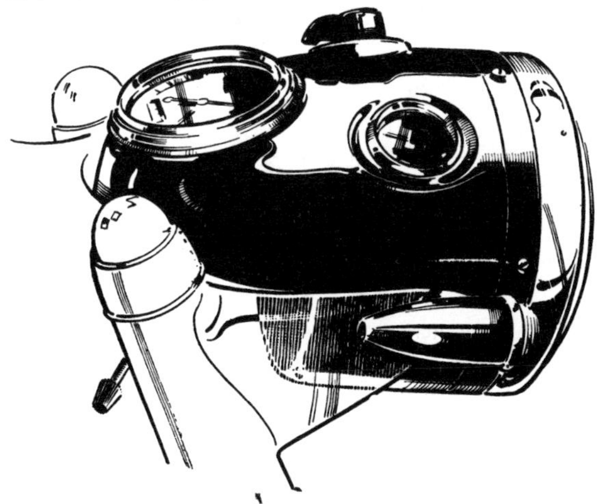

Fig 15 Lucas "Pre-focus" headlamp housing ammeter, lighting switch, and speedometer (1955–7)

*(By courtesy of "Motor Cycling" London)*

A "pre-focus" main bulb fits into a bulb holder at the rear of the reflector and is secured by a bayonet fixing adapter to which the three lighting cables are attached. The pilot or parking bulb below the main bulb is a push fit into the rear of the reflector.

To remove the lamp front (i.e. the light-unit assembly) to get access to the main and pilot bulbs, release the screw securing the lamp rim with one hand and support the light unit with the other. Then withdraw the light unit-assembly. Main bulb removal and fitting are effected as described later. To replace the light-unit assembly, engage the bottom tag on the lamp rim with the small slit in the lamp shield and gently press the top of the rim back into the lamp shell. Afterwards retighten the retaining screw on the top of the lamp body.

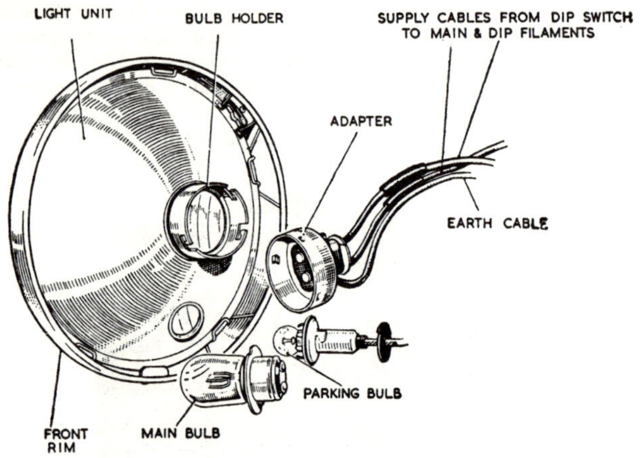


Fig 16 Light unit withdrawn from Lucas "Pre-focus" headlamp body (1958 onwards)

*(By courtesy of "Motor Cycling" London)*

**Separating Light Unit from Rim.** On all Lucas 1955–66 type headlamps, the front glass and reflector are made as one assembly (the "light unit") and cannot be separated. The light unit, however, can be removed from the chromium-plated rim by disengaging the spring clips from the turned-up inner edge of the rim by pressing them with the blade of a screwdriver, working away from the edge.

To fit the light-unit assembly to the rim, lay the unit in the rim so that the location block on the unit engages the forked bracket on the rim, and then spring home the spring clips. See that they are spaced at equal distances around the rim.

**Headlamp Bulb Renewal.** Fit *genuine* Lucas bulbs if occasion arises to renew them, and do not defer renewal until actual bulb failure occurs.

When fitting a "pre-focus" bulb (*see* Fig. 16) turn the back shell anti-clockwise and withdraw it. You can then remove the bulb from the holder in the back of the reflector. Insert the correct Lucas type bulb replacement in the bulb holder with its locating flange positioned, engage the projections on the inside of the adapter with the slots in the bulb holder, press on, and secure by turning clockwise.

**Correct Bulb Renewals.** The 1955–66 headlamps ("pre-focus" type) require a No. 312 (30/24-watt) Lucas double-filament main bulb which has a broad locating flange on the cap. An alternative bulb to the 6-volt No. 312 is the No. 373 (6-volt, 30/24-watt) Lucas double filament bulb. Both bulbs are suitable for "pre-focus" lamps with block lens light units, but the No. 373 bulb has a left-hand dip and is now recommended by the manufacturers for use in Great Britain. On continental models fit a Lucas No. 403 (6-volt, 35/35-watt) double filament-bulb which has a vertical dip. All 1955–66 headlamps require a No. 988 pilot bulb. 1955 and later Lucas stop-tail lamps require a 6-volt, 18/6-watt, No. 384 double-filament bulb. The correct speedometer bulb is a 6-volt, 1·8-watt No. 53205 M.C.C.

**The Ammeter.** 1955–66 models have the ammeter and lighting switch built into the Lucas headlamp as shown in Fig. 15. It indicates the amount of current flowing into or from the battery. If no charge is shown with the engine running and the lamps switched off, obviously the dynamo or the alternator is for some reason not charging the battery. Do not meddle with the ammeter. If its needle sticks or "flutters," take the motor-cycle to the nearest Lucas service depot.

**Cleaning Lucas Lamps.** Being situated high up, a headlamp seldom becomes dirty, but keep the glass clean. Polish the enamelled surface of the headlamp body with a good wax polish and a soft duster. The chromium plated rim should be cleaned with a damp chamois leather and afterwards polished with a soft duster. Note that on 1955 and later "sealed beam" Lucas headlamps (with Lucas light unit) the reflector cannot be detached for cleaning.

**Stop-tail Lamps.** 1955 and later A.M.C. machines have Lucas stop-tail lamps of type 564. The lamp has a double-filament 6-volt, 6/18-watt bulb; the 6-watt filament serves as the normal rear light and the 18-watt filament is illuminated only when the rear-brake pedal is depressed. To obtain access to the bulb it is only necessary to remove two screws and withdraw the thermoplastic cover. To prevent incorrect fitting of the No. 384 bulb, its securing pins are off-set. The bulb has a small bayonet cap.

## MAINTENANCE OF BATTERY (LEAD ACID)

Neglect of the battery quickly brings trouble, and correct attention in regard to its maintenance is *vitally* important. Upon it depend the lamps and horn.

**Topping-up the Cells.** Examine the acid level about every two weeks, and even more frequently in tropical climates. Unscrew the battery clamping-screw and remove the battery after first disconnecting the battery positive, negative leads. On 1955–65 models the Lucas battery is housed in a front compartment of the tool box.

To remove the battery on 1955–6 models, first release the rubber strap by grasping the loop attached to its lower end; pull downwards until the strap and loop are freed from the retaining clip at the platform base, and permit the rubber strap to slacken. Then lift the battery out.

To remove the battery on 1957–66 models, grasp the rubber strap with the fingers between the battery case and rubber strap. Push the strap downwards until it is possible to free the metal toggle from the strap retaining-clip, then carefully take the battery out.

Take off the battery lid and remove the three vent plugs. Inspect the hole in each vent plug and make certain that it is not obstructed. A choked vent plug hole will result in an increase of pressure in the cell owing to "gassing," and this may case trouble.

Wipe the top of the battery clean with a rag and also verify that the washer (where fitted) beneath each vent plug, to prevent leakage, is in position. After wiping the top of the battery, either destroy the rag or wash it thoroughly, using several changes of water. See that a supply of clean distilled water is to hand. Topping-up is necessary because the distilled water, unlike the acid, is gradually lost through evaporation.

Be careful not to hold a naked light near the vents. If the level is below the tops of the separators, add *distilled* water as required to bring the electrolyte level correct. This should be done just *before* a charge run, as the agitation due to running and the gassing will thoroughly mix the solution. Acid must not be added to the electrolyte unless the solution has been spilled. If the solution has been spilled by accident, add diluted sulphuric acid of specific gravity equal to that in the cells.

Undoubtedly the best way to top-up a battery without a correct-acid-level device is to use a Lucas battery filler. Insert its nozzle into each cell with the nozzle resting on the separators. Hold the battery filler in this position until air bubbles cease to rise in the glass container. The electrolyte level should then be correct, but examine it to make sure.

On 1955–66 machines with the PU7E/9 or PU7E/11 battery, pour distilled water round the flange (not the tube) of the acid-level device (*see* Fig. 17) until it stops draining into the cell. Then lift the tube slightly to enable the small amount of water in the flange to drain into the cell. The electrolyte level should then be correct. Inspect to make certain.

If the battery needs to be topped-up very often, possibly the C.V.C. unit needs to be adjusted (1955–7); if one cell requires more frequent topping-up than the others, probably the battery case, or container, is cracked, and battery renewal is called for. The carrier should also be cleaned up.

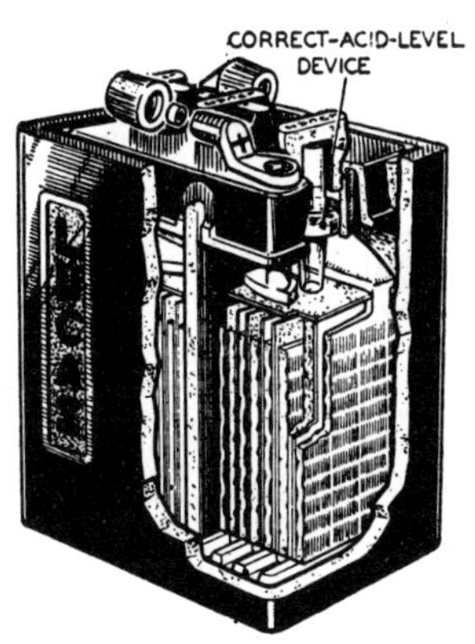


Fig 17 Keep the electrolyte level with the tops of the plate separators

*The battery shown is the Lucas PU7E/11 or PU7E with correct-acid-level device, fitted to many 1956–66 models. The PU7E/9 battery fitted to 1955 models is similar except for modified terminals and the omission of external cell connectors.*

**Checking Specific Gravity.** Very occasionally, hydrometer readings (specific gravity values) should be taken of the solution in each of the cells. The method of doing this is shown in Fig. 20. The Lucas hydrometer contains a graduated float which indicates the specific gravity (S.G.) of the battery cell from which a sample of electrolyte is taken.

After a sample has been taken and checked, it must, of course, be returned to the cell. The taking of S.G. readings with a hydrometer is the most efficient way of ascertaining the state of charge of the battery. The S.G. readings should be approximately the *same for all three cells*. Should the reading for one cell differ substantially from the readings for the others, probably some acid has been spilled or has leaked from the cell concerned. There is also a possibility of a short-circuit between the battery plates. In the latter case it will be necessary to return the battery to a Lucas service depot for attention.

Under no circumstances must the battery be permitted to remain in a discharged condition for long, or serious deterioration will occur. After checking the S.G. readings and topping-up the cells, wipe the top of the battery and remove any spilled electrolyte or water; replace the three vent plugs and the battery lid. Then fit and firmly secure the battery by means of the rubber strap referred to on page 42.

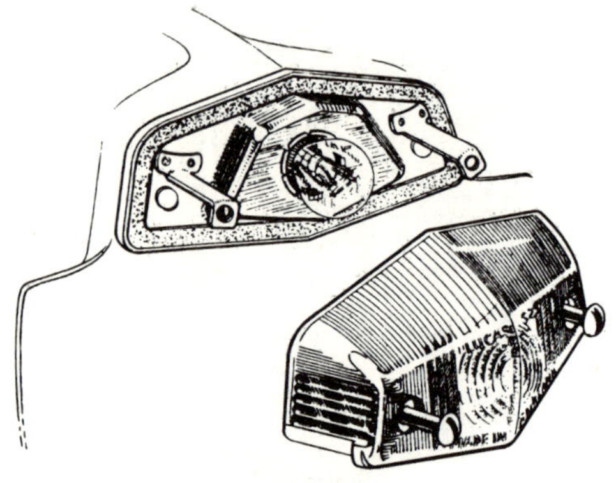


Fig 18 Lucas 525 stop-tail lamp

**Battery Connections.** Always keep the battery connections clean, free from corrosion, and tight, otherwise the ammeter readings will *not* indicate the true state of charge of the battery and proper battery charging may not occur.

**Correct Readings.** With Lucas batteries fitted to A.M.C. machines, the specific readings at an acid temperature of approximately 60°F should be: 1·270–1·290, battery fully charged; about 1·190–1·210 battery about half discharged; 1·110–1·130 battery fully discharged. If the temperature exceeds 60°F, add 0·002 to the hydrometer reading for each 5 degree rise in temperature above 60°F. Similarly if the temperature is below 60°F, deduct 0·002 for each 5 degrees decrease in temperature.

Never leave the battery in a discharged state for any appreciable period. If the machine is out of use, give the battery a freshening charge about once a fortnight. A low state of charge often is caused through parking the machine for long periods with the lighting switch in the "L" position, unaccompanied by much daylight running. The remedy is, of course, to undertake more daylight running and to keep the switch in the "Off" position as much as possible until the battery regains its normal state of charge. If overcharging occurs, have the setting of the compensated-voltage-control unit checked in the case of 1955–7 models.

**Battery Charging.** On 1955–7 models the compensated-voltage-control unit (*see* page 48) sees to it that the dynamo output is automatically controlled. On 1958–66 models the output of the alternator depends on the lighting switch position (*see* page 52).

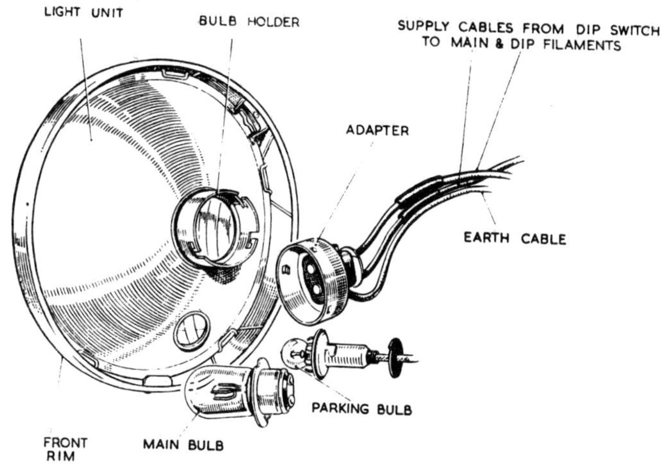


Fig 19 Light unit, main bulb and pilot, "Pre-focus" headlamp (1956–8 Norton 19, ES2, 50)

## MAINTENANCE OF DYNAMO (1955–7)

It is not necessary to take any special precautions when merely inspecting the commutator, but on making adjustments to the wiring circuit, it is essential to take steps to prevent accidental "shorting." Disconnect the lead from the lighting switch at the battery *negative* terminal. Push back the rubber shield and then unscrew the cable connector (where fitted). When doing this be sure that the cable does not make contact with any metal part of the frame, otherwise a "fat" spark will indicate that the battery *was* well charged! When reconnecting the lead, pull the rubber shield well over the connector.

**Lucas Servicing Advised.** It is a good plan every 10,000–15,000 miles to entrust the dynamo to a Lucas service depot for dismantling, cleaning, servicing, and lubrication. Lubrication is referred to on page 19.

**Inspection of Commutator and Brushgear.** The Lucas E3AR and the E3LM dynamos will run satisfactorily for thousands of miles without attention other than occasional inspection of the commutator and brush-gear. It is advisable, about every 5000–6000 miles, to remove the metal cover-band from the dynamo and make a careful inspection.

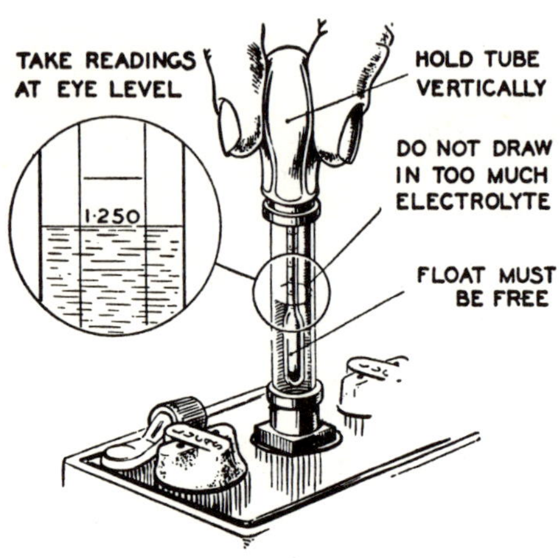


Fig 20 Use Lucas hydrometer to check specific gravity of electrolyte

**The Commutator Brushes.** The brushes must make good electrical contact with the commutator. They must be absolutely clean and able to move freely in their box-type holders, on holding back the retaining springs and gently pulling the leads and then releasing them. There must also be perfect contact between the brushes and the copper segments of the commutator; the brush faces in contact with the segments should be uniformly polished. Clean the brushes with a petrol-moistened cloth after removing them. To do this, pull back each brush-retaining spring (*see* Fig. 21) and remove the brush by pulling on its lead, being careful to see that the brush pressure-spring is clear of the brush holder.

Examine the carbon brushes for wear and unevenness, and true them up if necessary. Generally it is best to renew the brushes *before* serious wear develops, as this prevents sparking, which causes blackening of the commutator and an unsteady charging current. Always replace brushes in their original positions.

If Lucas brushes become so badly worn that it is necessary to remove them, this can easily be done as follows: Release the eyelet on the brush lead by unscrewing the hexagonal nut or screw at the terminal; then, holding back the spring level out of the way, withdraw the brush from its holder. Renew with genuine Lucas brushes.

The brush springs should be inspected occasionally to see that they have sufficient tension to keep the brushes firmly pressed against the commutator when the dynamo is running. It is particularly necessary to keep this in mind when the brushes have been in use a long time and are very much worn down.

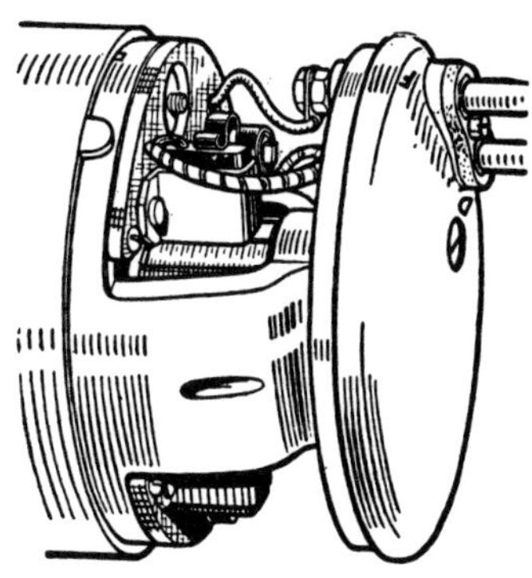

Fig 21 Commutator end of Lucas E3LM Dynamo with cover band removed

It is unwise to insert brushes of a grade other than that supplied with the dynamo, or to change the tension springs. The arrangement provided has been made only after many years' experience, and will be found to give the best results and the longest life. It is really best when the brushes become so worn that they no longer bed down on the commutator, or their flexible leads are exposed on their running faces, to have new brushes fitted at a Lucas service depot, as this ensures the brushes being properly "bedded."

**The Commutator.** The surface of the commutator segments should be kept clean and free from oil or brush dust, etc. Should any grease or oil work its way on to the commutator through over-lubrication, it will cause not only sparking, but, in addition, carbon and copper dust will collect in the grooves between the commutator segments.

The best way to clean the commutator is, without disconnecting any leads, to remove from its box-holder one of the main brushes and, inserting a fine dry duster, hold it, with a suitably-shaped piece of wood, against the commutator surface, causing the armature to be rotated by the kick-starter. Slow rotation is assisted by removing the sparking plug. If the commutator is very dirty, first moisten the cloth with petrol. The segments should be *dark bronze* and highly polished.

**To Adjust Dynamo Chain.** The tension of the dynamo chain which lies behind the primary chain (*see* Fig. 53) should be checked occasionally, after removing the oil-bath case inspection cap (*see* page 22). Chain whip with the chain in its tightest position, mid-way between the sprockets, should be approximately ¼ in.

To make an eccentric adjustment for chain tension, first slacken the strap bolt clamping the dynamo in its housing. Now rotate the dynamo *anti-clockwise* (with the fingers, 1955–7 models) until chain tension is felt to be correct on passing a finger through the inspection-cap opening. Be careful not to confuse the primary chain with the dynamo chain which lies *behind* the former (*see* Fig. 57). Afterwards retighten the strap bolt and again check the tension of the dynamo chain. If found to be correct, replace the inspection cap on the oil-bath chain case (*see* page 22).

**Compensated Voltage Control.** All 1955–7 A.M.C. motor-cycles incorporate compensated-voltage-control. The C.V.C. unit consists of a cut-out and voltage regulator unit in a box beneath the saddle, beside the battery carrier, or (1956–7) in the tool box. It is connected between the dynamo and battery and sees to it that the battery is automatically charged the right amount by varying the dynamo output according to the state of charge of the battery and the load imposed on it.

Current is prevented from flowing back from the battery to the dynamo at low r.p.m. by means of the cut-out which opens. As soon as the r.p.m. rise high enough to enable the dynamo to charge the battery, the cut-out closes and completes the circuit.

In all three lighting switch positions (*see* page 52) the dynamo gives a controlled output and thus relieves you of responsibility in regard to charging. The regulator begins to operate when the dynamo voltage reaches about 7·3 volts. During daylight running with the battery well charged and the switch in the "Off" position, the dynamo gives only a trickle charge, and the ammeter reading is unlikely to exceed 1–2 amp. There is no danger of overcharging.

The regulator provides for an increase of dynamo output as soon as the lamps are switched on. The effect of switching the lamps on after a long run with the battery voltage high is often to cause a temporary discharge reading at the ammeter, but fairly soon the voltage falls and the regulator responds, thereby causing the output of the dynamo to balance the load of the lamps.

When the battery is in a discharged state, the regulator increases the dynamo output and restores the battery to its normal state of charge in the shortest possible time.

**Do Not Tamper with C.V.C. Unit.** The unit is sealed by the makers, as it should not need adjustment once it is correctly set. If, however, the battery (in good condition) is persistently under-charged or over-charged, suspect the C.V.C. unit setting and have it checked, preferably at a Lucas service depot. Note that the C.V.C. unit is retained by self-locking nuts, except on 1956–7 models where it is retained in a sponge-rubber holder in a partition at the rear top-corner of the tool box (see Fig. 16). To remove the C.V.C. unit on a 1956–7 model, grasp it between the fingers and thumb of one hand, and gently and firmly pull it away from the rubber holder.

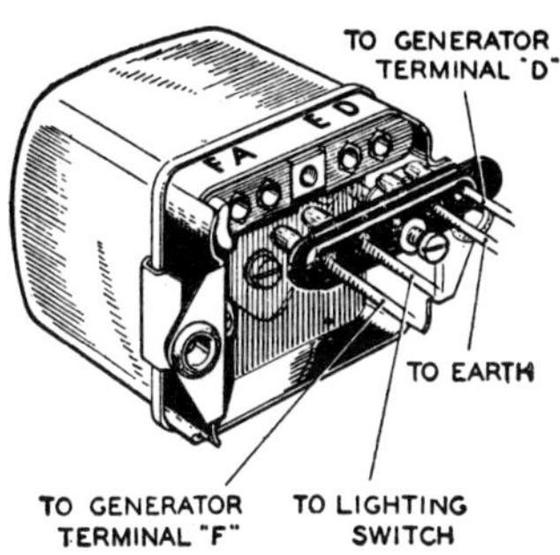


Fig 22 Connections to compensated voltage-control unit

As may be seen in Fig. 22, the four terminals of the C.V.C. unit are clearly marked by the letters F.A.E.D. Leads from the *F* and *D* terminals are attached to similarly marked terminals on the dynamo. The terminal marked *A* is connected to one of the switch terminals, and the terminal marked *E* is earthed.

**To Remove the Dynamo (1955–7).** On machines with the magneto positioned in front of the engine, dynamo removal is very straightforward and no retiming of the magneto is necessary.

First remove the near-side footrest arm. Lay a drip-tray beneath the oil-bath chain case to receive the oil, and remove the outer portion of the oil-bath chain case (*see* page 109). Next remove the spring circlip, the locking plate, and the nut securing the dynamo sprocket, and with a suitable tool withdraw the sprocket. While slackening the sprocket-retaining nut, hold the sprocket with the appropriate spanner (Part No. 017254). This prevents any bending stress being imposed on the spindle of the dynamo.

Disconnect the dynamo leads and slacken the dynamo clamping-bolt fully. Now twist the dynamo by hand until the locating strip on its body aligns with the key-way cut-away in the rear engine plate housing the dynamo. Then withdraw the dynamo, tilting it upwards so as to clear the gearbox.

**To Replace the Dynamo (1955–7).** Observe the removal instructions in reverse. Be careful to locate the dynamo-sprocket key accurately when fitting the dynamo sprocket. Also check that the dynamo chain is correctly tensioned (*see* page 48), and follow the instructions given (page 110) for replacing the outer half of the oil-bath chain case. Before fitting this outer half, make sure that the dynamo sprocket securing-nut is firmly tightened prior to the fitting of the locking plate and the retaining circlip.

**Removal of Dynamo Chain (1955–7 Models).** First remove the outer half of the oil-bath chain case (*see* page 109). Next remove the nut retaining the engine sprocket. This is facilitated by engaging top gear and applying the rear brake. Withdraw the shock-absorber spring, cupped washer, and cam. Now remove the primary chain to obtain access to the dynamo chain (*see* Fig. 57). Remove the spring circlip from the nut retaining the sprocket on the dynamo armature. Also detach the locking washer or plate which surrounds the nut. With the appropriate spanner (Part No. 017254) applied to the two flats on the back of the dynamo sprocket, hold the sprocket and unscrew the dynamo sprocket retaining-nut. With a suitable extractor tool release the dynamo sprocket from the armature. Now remove in one operation the dynamo sprocket, "endless" dynamo chain, and the engine sprocket assembly.

**Replacing Dynamo Sprocket, Chain, and Engine Sprocket (1955–7).** Check that the key for the dynamo sprocket is in position on the armature location. Also verify that the spacing collar (between the crankcase ball bearing and the back of the engine sprocket) is replaced on the engine driving-side mainshaft. Next engage the dynamo driving chain with the teeth of the dynamo driving sprocket (the smaller sprocket of the engine-sprocket assembly) and the sprocket which fits on the dynamo armature. In one simultaneous operation replace the two sprockets (and chain) on the engine mainshaft and dynamo armature. Then replace the plain washer and sprocket retaining nut on the dynamo armature. Tighten the nut finger-tight only.

While preventing the dynamo armature from turning by applying the appropriate spanner (Part No. 017254) to the flats on the back of the sprocket, tighten the dynamo sprocket retaining nut firmly. Replace the locking washer or plate for the retaining nut, also the retaining circlip. Make sure that the latter beds down properly in the nut groove. Finally replace the cam of the engine shaft shock-absorber, the spring, cap washer, and retaining nut. Also replace the primary chain and check its tension (*see* page 101). The outer half of the oil-bath chain case can now be replaced (*see* pages 110–12).

## THE ALTERNATOR AND RECTIFIER (1958–66)

**The Lucas RM15, RM19 Alternator.** This on 1958–66 models comprises a spigot-mounted 6-coil laminated stator bolted to the oil-bath chain case cover (*see* Fig. 58), with a rotor carried on and driven by an extension of the crankshaft. The aluminium rotor has a hexagonal steel core, each face of which carries a permanent magnet keyed to a laminated pole tip.

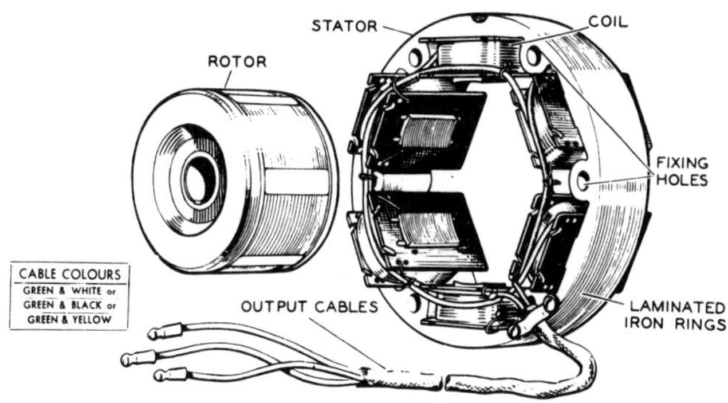


Fig 23 Lucas alternator RM15/RM19

Because, unlike the Lucas dynamos fitted to 1955–7 models, the alternator and stator have no rotating windings, commutator, brushgear, bearings, or oil seals, no maintenance whatever is called for other than to see that the three snap-connections in the output cables (*see* Fig. 23) are tight and clean, and the leads unfrayed. The snap-connections, by the way, are located behind the frame cover which is secured by two knurled screws.

Should it be necessary for any reason to withdraw the rotor, there is no need to fit keepers to the rotor poles. After removing a rotor wipe off any metal swarf which may have collected on the pole tips. Place the rotor in a clean place.

**To Remove A.C. Rotor.** The rotor is keyed to the engine shaft. If removal is required for some reason, first remove the outer half of the oil-bath chain case (*see* page 109). Next engage top gear and apply pressure to the rear brake pedal. Then unscrew the lock-nut and the nut securing the rotor. Withdraw the washer and pull off the rotor.

**The Alternator Output Control.** While riding normally with the ignition switch in the "ON" position the rate of output depends on the position of the lighting switch, electrical energy passing through the battery from the alternator in the form of rectified alternating current.

When the lighting switch is turned to the "OFF" position the alternator output supplies the ignition coil and trickle-charges the battery. When the lighting switch is turned to the "L" or "H" position the alternator output is automatically increased to meet the extra load.

**Altering the Alternator Connections.** In the event of the battery becoming discharged it is possible to effect a temporary boost by altering the alternator connections behind the frame cover after removing the two knurled screws and removing the cover. Alter the connections in the following manner.

On 1958–60 models disconnect the green and yellow and dark green connectors. Reconnect the dark green cable connector to the green and yellow cable connector. Do not interfere with the light green cable.

On 1961–6 models disconnect the green and yellow and green and black connectors. Reconnect the green and black to the green and yellow. Do not interfere with the green and white cable.

Note that prolonged use of the machine with the alternator connections altered is not recommended and will *harm the battery*.

**The Lucas Rectifier.** The Lucas rectifier is housed on the tool-box below the dualseat. The rectifier consists of four plates (coated on one side with selenium) and functions like a non-return valve, permitting current to pass in one direction only. The alternating current from the alternator is thus converted to unidirectional (d.c.) current for charging the battery. The rectifier needs no maintenance other than to keep the connections clean and tight, and to check periodically that the nut securing the rectifier to the frame of the motor-cycle is tight. *Do not in any circumstances loosen the nut which clamps the rectifier plates together*. The nut is most carefully adjusted during manufacture to give optimum performance.

**The Rectifier Connections.** Should the leads be disconnected from the rectifier it is vital to see that they are reconnected correctly. Fig. 24 shows how the coloured cables should be connected to 1958–66 rectifiers. Never alter this arrangement.

## THE ELECTRIC HORN

Careful adjustment of the Lucas horn is made at the works, and subsequent adjustment is rarely called for. Normally the horn should give long service without any attention whatsoever. The vibrating parts do, however, gradually wear and, after very considerable usage, some roughness and loss of tone may develop. This necessitates an examination being made at a Lucas service depot.

**If Horn Fails Completely or Partially.** Do not immediately infer that the horn has broken down or needs adjustment. Possible causes of the trouble are: a loose fixing bolt; vibration of some adjacent part; a discharged battery; a loose connection; a short circuit in the wiring; or a defective push-switch. The last-mentioned may be occasioned through poor electrical contact with the handlebars.

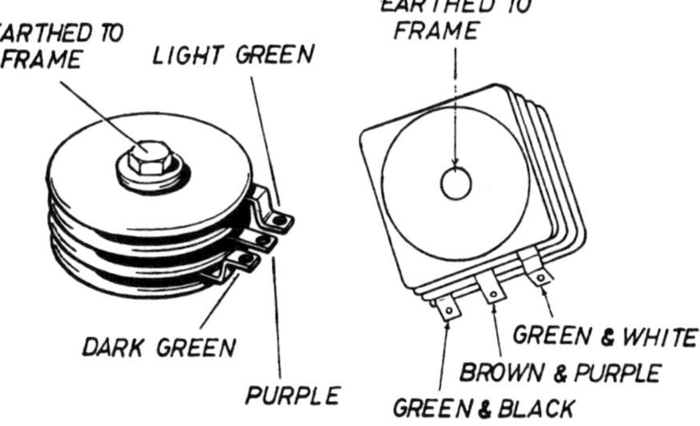


Fig 24 The Lucas rectifiers showing connections

*The rectifier shown on the left is fitted to* **1958–60** *models. That on the right is fitted to* **1961–5** *models.*

## THE WIRING CIRCUIT (1955–66)

**No Fuse Provided.** There is no fuse incorporated in the wiring circuit, which is purposely simplified, and capable of being understood by those with elementary electrical knowledge. If care is taken to keep the various wires correctly connected, and to maintain the connections clean and firm, there is no risk of an excessive current damaging any of the equipment or wiring.

**Occasionally Inspect the Wiring.** It is advisable occasionally to make a careful inspection of the wiring, especially of the wires from the battery, the leads from the dynamo to the C.V.C. unit or the alternator output cables (1958–66). See that the insulation is sound and not chafed and that all connections are clean and tight. Should a dynamo fail to charge, this may be due to dynamo trouble, a faulty lead, or a faulty C.V.C unit. Tape up any loose or frayed leads.

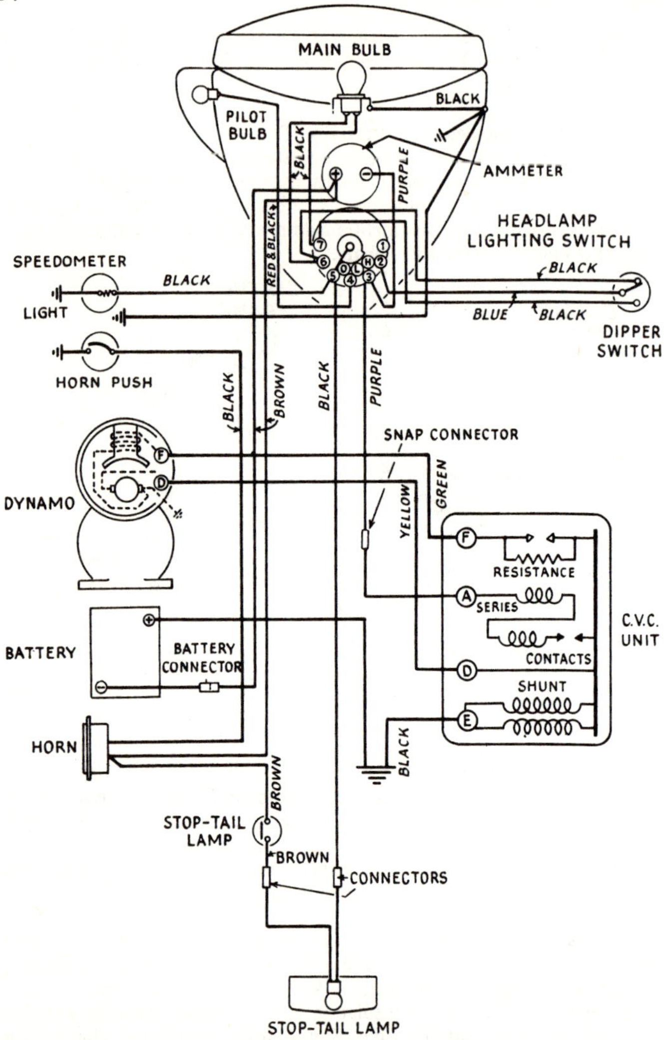


Fig 25 Wiring diagram for Lucas "Magdyno" lighting with SSU7OOP/1 headlamp (1955–7 models)

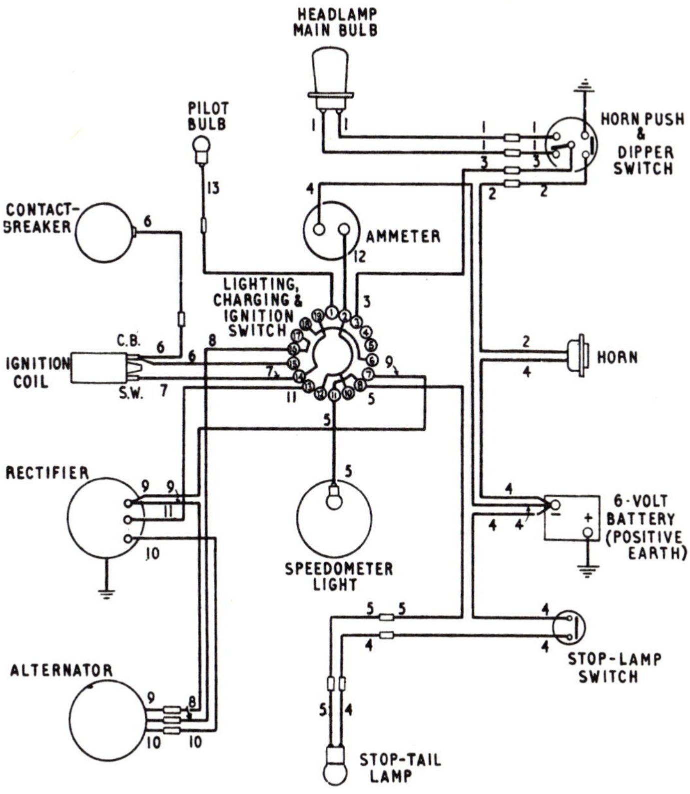


Fig 26 Wiring diagram for all 1958–9 models (positive earth)

**KEY TO SLEEVE COLOURS**

1. *Black*
2. *Brown and black*
3. *Blue*
4. *Brown and blue*
5. *Brown and green*
6. *Black and white*
7. *White*
8. *Green and yellow*
9. *Dark green*
10. *Light green*
11. *Purple*
12. *Brown and white*
13. *Red*

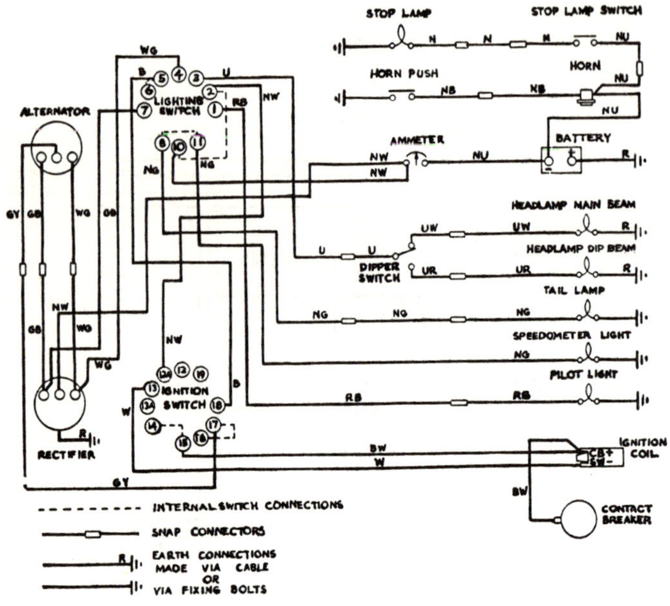


Fig 27 Wiring diagram for all 1960–6 models (positive earth)

**KEY TO SLEEVE COLOURS**

| | |
|---|---|
| B. *Black* | R. *Red* |
| G. *Green* | U. *Blue* |
| L. *Light* | W. *White* |
| N. *Brown* | Y. *Yellow* |
| P. *Purple* | |

As may be seen in Figs. 24–28, the ends of leads can be identified for connection purposes by means of their coloured sleeves. This greatly facilitates reconnecting the wiring circuit in the event of the wires being disconnected from the various terminals.

The leads connected to the terminals marked "*D*" and "*F*" on a dynamo and C.V.C. unit must on no account be reversed. To prevent this being done, the screw in the dynamo terminal block is off-centre, and the screws securing the regulator clamping plate are of different size.

**Important Precaution.** It is extremely important to disconnect one of the battery leads (*see* page 45) if making any alterations to the wiring or

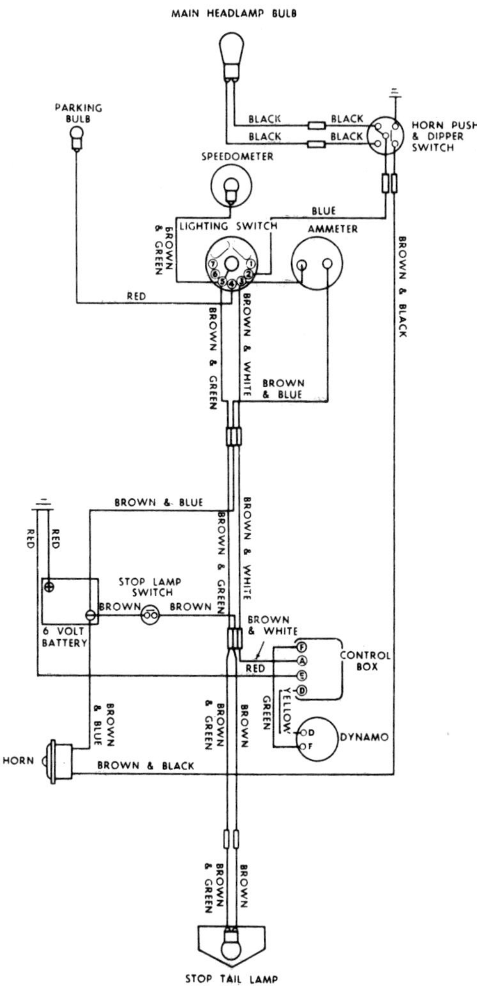


Fig 28 Wiring diagram for Lucas "Magdyno" lighting equipment with MCH58 headlamp

*This applies to* 1956–8 *Norton models* 19, *ES2*, 50.

removing the lighting switch from the Lucas headlamp. *On all 1955–66 models the battery positive terminal is earthed*. The earth connection is connected to the dualseat lug tube. The dualseat must be removed to obtain access to it.

**The Battery Lead Connections.** On all later (MLZ9E, PUZ7E type) Lucas batteries detachable lead-connectors are provided at the battery terminals. To make a lead connection, unscrew the knurled terminal nut and withdraw the collet or cone-shaped insert. Note that the inserts for the two terminals are not interchangeable. After baring the lead end for about an inch, thread the bared end through the knurled nut and collet. Then insert the collet and cable into the terminal after first bending the wire strands over the narrow end of the collet. Tighten the knurled nut firmly to secure the connection.

# 5 General Maintenance

Some aspects of motor-cycle maintenance have already been dealt with in the preceding chapters. Consequently this chapter contains only cross-references to such matters. Full instructions are given in respect of maintenance operations not previously covered.

**Spares and Repairs.** It is essential when you have occasion to forward or deliver parts to spares stockists (either for repair or as patterns) to attach to *each* part a label on which is written clearly your full name and address. To ensure quick attention, all correspondence concerning spares and technical advice should be written on separate sheets, each bearing your name and address.

Always quote the *complete* engine number or frame number, according to the nature of the part involved. The frame number will be found marked on the right-hand side of the seat lug below the saddle (on main frame head lug, 1958–66). The engine number (with letter prefix) will be found on the left-hand side of the crankcase.

There are numerous firms in the United Kingdom who can supply motor-cycle spares over the counter, and also many who specialize in the repair of engines and gearboxes. Useful addresses may be found in the advertisement pages of *Motor Cycle*. If taking a machine to Norton Villiers Ltd. first make an appointment. Their address is North Way, Walworth Industrial Estate, Andover, Hants.

**Some Large Accessory Firms.** Among reputable London firms (some of which have provincial branches) handling motor-cycle accessories, equipment, proprietary spares, tools, clothing, etc., may be mentioned: Whitbys of Acton, Ltd.; Claude Rye, Ltd.; E. S. Motors; The Halford Cycle Co., Ltd.; Turner's Stores; James Grose, Ltd.; Marble Arch Motor Supplies, Ltd.; Pride & Clark, Ltd.; and George Grose, Ltd.

## ENGINE MAINTENANCE

**Necessary Items for Maintenance.** For engine maintenance there are certain items which you *must* have handy in the lock-up or garage. These include: a can of paraffin for cleaning purposes; a stiff brush for scouring dirt off the crankcase; a tin of suitable engine oil (*see* page 13); a canister of grease; a small oil-can containing some engine oil; a receptacle for oil when draining the oil tank and oil sump; a pail or some jars for washing engine parts in; some non-fluffy rags; valve grinding paste such as Richford's (coarse and fine); some fine emery-cloth; a set of engine gaskets (*see* illustrated Spares List); some jointing compound; a pair of new gudgeon-pin circlips; and some good hand cleanser.

**Tools for the Job.** The comprehensive A.M.C. tool kit is adequate for any normal stripping down and assembly job and should prove sufficient for routine maintenance and overhaul. It is also necessary for maintenance to obtain a suitable feeler gauge for checking the sparking plug gap (*see* page 62), a valve-spring compressor (for 1955 and subsequent engines with hairpin valve springs), and a valve holder for grinding-in the valves. The Part Nos. are 018276 and 017482 respectively. It is also desirable to obtain a wire brush for cleaning sparking plugs.

Should you decide to undertake as much repair work as possible in addition to routine maintenance, stripping-down, and assembly, it is desirable to rig up a suitable bench, complete with vice, and to purchase some extra tools (various service tools are available). Repair work is beyond the scope of this handbook, and you are not advised to tackle such work unless you have fair technical knowledge and skill in handling tools.

**Lubrication of Engine.** Detailed instructions on lubricating the A.M.C. engine and the care of the dry-sump lubrication system are given in Chapter 2. Attend to lubrication points 1 to 4 indicated in the Lubrication Chart on page 21.

**The Amal Carburettor.** For comprehensive advice on how to obtain and maintain correct carburation, refer to the instructions given in Chapter 3.

**Keep the Engine Clean.** Keep your engine clean externally as well as internally. By so doing you enhance pride of ownership and obtain other advantages. Dirt is apt to mask defects and can accidentally enter the engine when it is being stripped down. It will also make rusting more likely. Rusted cylinder fins, besides being an eyesore, are detrimental to efficient dispersion of heat by radiation. They should be clean and black. 1955–66 models have light-alloy cylinder heads.

To clean the cylinder and cylinder-head fins, use a stiff brush dipped in paraffin. If the stove-enamelling has worn away, paint the fins with a good proprietary cylinder black. Clean the aluminium alloy and bright surfaces with rags and paraffin, assisted by brushes where necessary, and scour off the filth from the lower part of the crankcase by means of stiff brushes and paraffin. Thorough cleaning may take some time, but it is well worthwhile.

**Check Nuts for Tightness Occasionally.** On a new machine where some initial bedding-down occurs, it is advisable to check all external nuts and bolts for tightness fairly frequently. After the running-in period is completed, it is a good habit to check the external nuts regularly every 3000 miles. Pay special attention to the cylinder nuts, the nuts on the engine plates, and the union nuts for the pipe connections.

## CARE OF IGNITION SYSTEM

The ignition system comprises: a 14 mm sparking plug; a Lucas rotating-magnet type magneto (1955–7 models), with automatic ignition-control mechanism on the driving side; or a Lucas type CAIA contact-breaker unit with automatic timing control (1958 onwards). The contact-breaker unit and timing control are both housed in the timing case of the 1958 and later coil-ignition models. They are operated from the inlet camshaft, and a coil is clipped to the frame top tube underneath the petrol tank. Current is taken from the battery through the contact-breaker unit to the ignition coil (unless the ignition key is in the "EMG" position).

**Suitable Sparking Plugs.** To obtain maximum engine performance throughout the throttle range, plus easy starting, it is essential always to run on a suitable type of sparking plug. Four reliable makes of sparking plugs are the KLG, the Lodge, the Champion and the NGK. Suitable (14 mm thread and ¾ in. reach) types are—

KLG—Fit a three-point, detachable type FE80, or else the appropriate watertight version.

LODGE—Fit a three-point, detachable type HLN or a type HLNP on all 1955 and later models.

CHAMPION—Fit a non-detachable type N-5 (all 1955 and later models).

NGK—Fit a non-detachable type B-7E (all 1955–66 models). This has a *copper* centre electrode.

For regular bad-weather riding it is advisable to fit a weatherproof terminal cover to the plug, or else to use a watertight plug corresponding to the appropriate non-watertight plugs recommended above. "Suppressor" covers stop radio and television interference.

**Be Careful When Removing a Plug.** If considerable resistance is felt when removing a sparking plug with the usual box spanner and tommy bar, apply some penetrating oil to the plug threads. Do not forget that on 1955 and later models the cylinder head is made of a light alloy and the plug threads can be damaged if excessive force is used to remove the sparking plug. A cylinder head costs considerably more than a sparking plug!

**Checking the Plug Gap.** It is advisable to check the gap between the electrodes of the sparking plug about every 3000 miles. The correct gap is 0·020–0·022 in., and it is advisable to re-gap the plug if burning of the points has increased the gap to over 0·022 in. When re-gapping a plug it is desirable for obvious reasons to set its gap at or near the *bottom* limit.

Check the gap with a suitable feeler gauge (a wire gauge if the points are not very accessible). The gauge should be a nice sliding fit. When adjusting

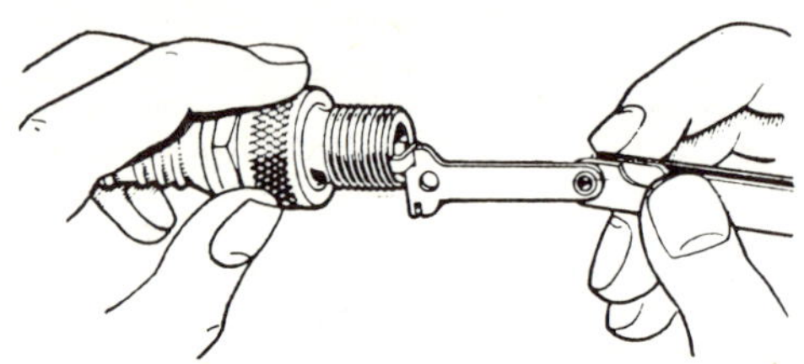

Fig 29 A safe method of re-gapping a plug using a Champion tool

the gap, never attempt to bend or tap the centre electrode. Use a plug re-gapping tool (*see* Fig. 29), a small pair of snipe-nose pliers, or a small screwdriver to bend the outside (earth) electrode(s). Tapping the outer electrode(s) inwards to reduce the gap is permissible, if the plug is held in a vice and a light hammer and copper drift are used. When the plug has to be thoroughly cleaned, this should be done as described below, and the plug re-gapped *afterwards*.

**Cleaning the Sparking Plug.** If carburation is quite satisfactory and excessive oil is not entering the combustion chamber, it should not be necessary to dismantle and clean the sparking plug thoroughly more often than once about every 3000 miles. When running-in a new or rebored engine, however, it is advisable to remove and check the plug for cleanliness at intervals of about 500 miles.

Quick cleaning of a plug can be done by brushing the points and lightly rubbing their firing sides with some smooth emery-cloth. Thorough cleaning (internal and external), however, is not possible without dismantling it or using garage equipment.

To clean the metal parts (plug body and gland nut), wipe them clean with petrol, or, if necessary, scrape off the deposits with a small knife, or use a wire brush. Afterwards rinse the parts in petrol. The gland nut seldom gets very fouled, but the inside of the plug body may be very dirty, and the same may apply to the external threads of the plug. Clean and polish the points of the centre and outside (earth) electrodes (*F*) and (*G*) with some fine glass-paper.

See that there is no dirt or grit lodged between the body of the plug and the insulation, and particularly on the internal sealing washer and all contacting faces. Smear a little thin oil on the internal washer and make sure that it seats properly. When assembling the sparking plug, see that the centre electrode and insulation are positioned centrally in the body bore. If they are not, remove, reposition by rotating the centre a quarter of a turn, and reassemble. Do not attempt to force the centre electrode into position or bend it.

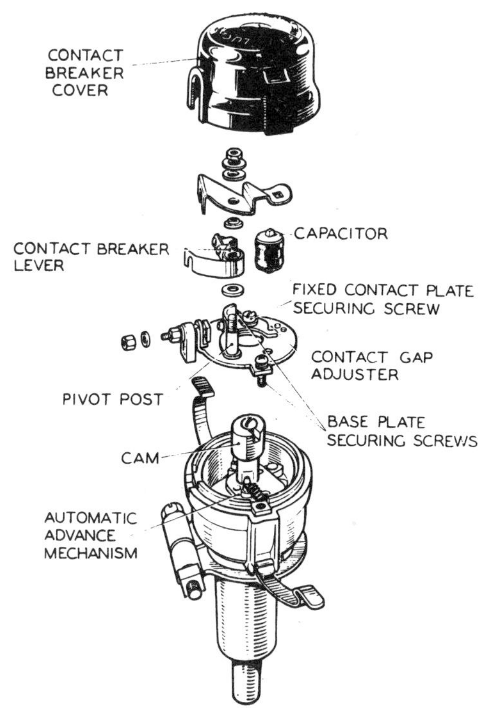


Fig 30 Contact-breaker unit (1959–62 Nortons) shown dismantled

*The operating cam and the auto-advance mechanism are shown. Correct gap is* **0·014–0·016 in.**

**Replacing the Sparking Plug.** Before replacing the plug, renew the copper washer if it is worn or flattened, and clean the plug threads. It is a good plan to coat the threads with some graphite paste before replacing the plug. Screw the plug home by hand as far as possible, and always use the plug box spanner in the tool kit for final tightening. The use of excessive force is undesirable and can cause distortion and possibly damage the cylinder-head threads.

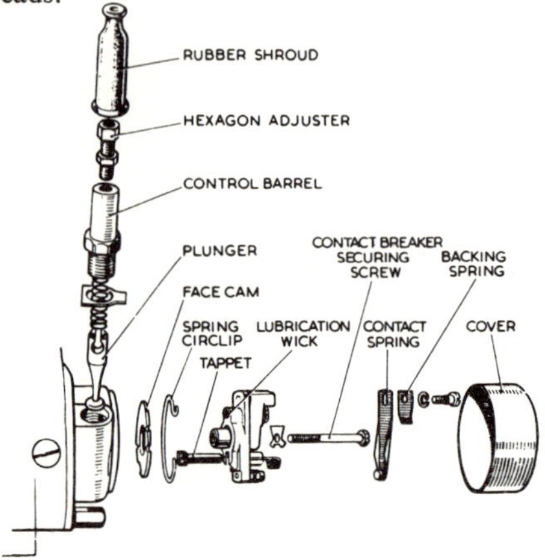

Fig 31 Contact-breaker and ignition control dismantled (1955–8 Norton)

**To Check Contact-breaker Gap (1955–7).** On 1955–7 models it is advisable after the first 500 miles to remove the moulded cover from the Lucas type S.R.–1 rotating-magnet magneto and check the gap between the contacts of the contact-breaker. It is subsequently sufficient to check the gap at intervals of about 3000 miles. Actual adjustment is seldom needed. The correct contact-breaker gap is 0·010–0·012 in.

The correct procedure for checking the contact-breaker gap is as follows—

1. Remove the contact-breaker cover and rotate the engine slowly forwards until the contacts of the contact-breaker are wide open.

2. Insert the blade of the feeler gauge (attached to the magneto spanner) between the contacts.

3. If the feeler gauge *just* slides in without friction, the gap is correct and no adjustment is needed. If the gauge is a slack fit or the contacts have to be sprung to enable it to enter, adjust the gap as below.

Should an adjustment of the contact-breaker gap be necessary, slacken the two securing screws (*see* Fig. 32) holding the fixed contact plate and move the plate as required until the gap is correct. Having made the required adjustment, firmly tighten the two securing-screws, again check the gap, and finally replace the moulded cover. Tighten its three fixing-screws firmly.

**To Check Contact-breaker Gap (1958 Onwards).** On the 1958 and later models check the contact-breaker gap after covering 500 miles on a new machine, and thereafter regularly about every 3000 miles.

To check the contact-breaker gap, first remove the two screws securing the outer cover to the timing case, and remove the cover. Next turn the engine over slowly until the contacts are fully open. Then insert a suitable

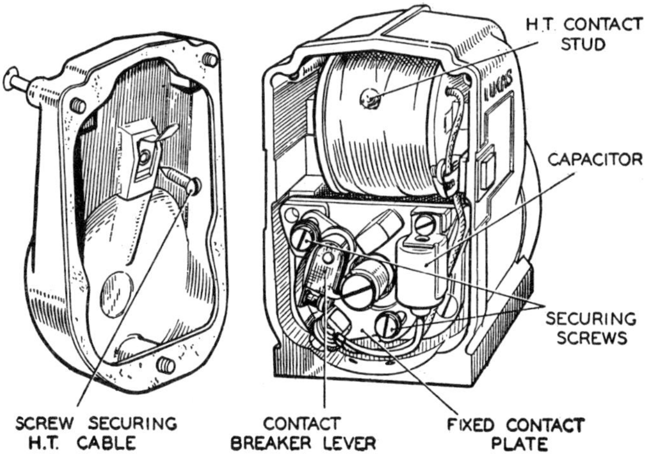


Fig 32 Contact-breaker end of Lucas rotating-magnet magneto (1955–7)

*This magneto has automatic ignition-control mechanism on the driving side.*

feeler gauge between the contacts and check the gap which should be 0·014–0·016 in. If the correct size feeler gauge just slides in without friction, the gap is correct and no adjustment is needed. If an adjustment is required, make it as described below.

With the engine still in the position where the maximum contact gap is obtained, loosen the two screws which secure the contact plate (8, Fig. 33). Then adjust the position of the plate as required until the gap between the contacts is correct. Afterwards fully tighten the two plate-securing screws.

**Keep the Contact-breaker Clean.** The contact-breaker, especially the contacts themselves, must *never* be permitted to get dirty or oily, otherwise ignition trouble will inevitably ensue, and the contacts will become burned and pitted. When checking the gap of the contact-breaker, on magneto and coil-ignition models, about every 3000 miles inspect the contacts closely, and if they need cleaning, do this *before* finally adjusting the gap.

If the contacts have a *grey*, *frosted* appearance, it can be reasonably assumed that they are fairly healthy. Should they be only slightly discoloured, clean both contacts with a cloth moistened with petrol. Where

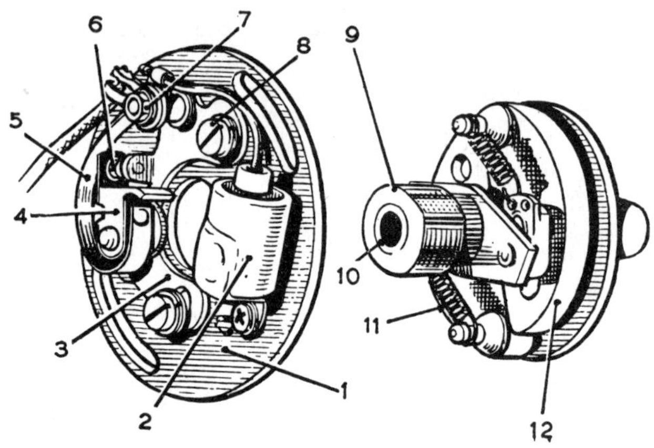


Fig 33 The contact-breaker (left) and automatic ignition-timing control (right) units removed from the timing-case cover and inlet camshaft of a coil-ignition model (1958–66)

1. *Contact-breaker plate*
2. *Capacitor*
3. *Contact plate (adjustable)*
4. *Contact-breaker lever*
5. *Spring for 4*
6. *Contacts*
7. *Terminal nut*
8. *Securing screw (one of two) for 1*
9. *Cam operating contact-breaker*
10. *Hole for bolt securing timing-control unit*
11. *Spring (one of two) controlling bob weight*
12. *Bob weight (one of two)*

the contacts are pitted or blackened, they must be thoroughly cleaned with a fine carborundum stone, or if one is not available, *very fine* emery-cloth. Afterwards all metallic dust and dirt must be completely removed with a petrol-moistened cloth.

When cleaning and dressing the contacts, it is essential to remove the minimum amount of contact metal necessary to ensure: (*a*) brightness of the contacts, (*b*) parallelism of the contacts, (*c*) perfect smoothness and truth of contact faces. To ensure this it is advisable to withdraw the moving contact.

**To Withdraw Moving Contact (1955–7).** On 1955–7 models with a rotating-magnet type magneto, to remove the contact-breaker lever (*see* Fig. 32) carrying the moving contact, remove the nut securing the end of the contact-breaker spring. The spring is slotted to permit of easy withdrawal of the lever.

**To Withdraw Moving Contact (1958–66).** To withdraw the moving contact on 1958 and later models having coil ignition, unscrew the nut which secures the end of the spring (*see* Fig. 33) and remove the nut, spring washer, and bush. Then lift the contact-breaker lever carrying the moving contact off its pivot.

**To Renew h.t. Cable (1955–7).** Where a Lucas rotating-magnet type SR–1 magneto is fitted, 7 mm rubber-covered type ignition cable is required for renewal purposes. To connect to the magneto, first remove the moulded cover from the contact-breaker side, and unscrew the pointed screw (*see* Fig. 32) from the back of the cover. Pull out the old ignition cable and push the new cable right home. Then secure the cable by tightening the pointed screw. Its point will penetrate the insulation and ensure good electrical contact with the core of the cable.

**Testing h.t. Cable at Plug.** If the engine is running well, obviously the cable is sound, but if the engine refuses to start, it is desirable to ascertain whether the h.t. current is reaching the plug end of the cable. Place the steel blade of a *wooden-handled* screwdriver in contact with the plug terminal and almost in contact with one of the cylinder fins. Kick the engine over smartly and note whether a "fat" spark occurs. If it does, the cable is sound, but if it does not, the cable or magneto is at fault.

**The Ignition Coil (1958 Onwards).** The Lucas type MA6 ignition coil is clipped to the frame top tube beneath the petrol tank. The coil requires no maintenance except keeping the connections tight and the coil exterior clean, particularly the terminals. When the high-tension cable shows signs of cracking or perishing, renew it with 7 mm Neoprene-covered or rubber-covered ignition cable; also renew the connectors. The high-tension cable can be pulled from the moulded terminal socket together with its connector.

**Retensioning Magneto Chain (1955–7).** About every 3000 miles remove the cover from the magneto chain-case and inspect the chain carefully for tension. Some stretching occurs, especially on a new chain, and where this is excessive it may spoil the exact ignition-timing and also accelerate wear of the chain and sprockets. Press the magneto chain-run up and down (in its *tautest* position) midway between the magneto and camshaft sprockets. If the tension is correct, the *total* deflection should not exceed approximately ¼ in. If it is appreciably more or less, retension the chain as described below. Over-tensioning may damage the magneto.

1. Loosen the nuts on both bolts (nut on rear bolt only, 1955–7) which support and secure the adjustable magneto platform.
2. Insert the blade of a screwdriver beneath the rear end of the magneto platform and prise it upwards until the correct chain tension is obtained.
3. Tighten firmly the single nut on the magneto-platform near securing bolt.
4. Again check the tension of the driving chain.
5. Grease the chain if necessary (*see* page 21) and fit the cover to the chain case. Do not use jointing compound. Tighten the various cover securing-screws evenly.

**Automatic Ignition-control Mechanism (1955–7).** The control mechanism on the driving side of the Lucas type SR–1 rotating-magnet magneto requires no adjustment, but the mechanism should be greased (*see* page 21) when greasing the magneto chain.

**Automatic Ignition-control Unit Removal (1958–66).** Normally the unit requires no attention other than occasional lubrication (*see* page 18). Removal is therefore unlikely to be necessary unless the renewal of some part is required after an extremely big mileage. Removal is necessary, however, as a preliminary to retiming the ignition on coil-ignition models. The following is the correct procedure.

First remove the outer cover from the timing case after removing the two securing screws. Next remove the two securing screws which pass through slotted holes in the fixed contact-breaker plate (*see* Fig. 33) and remove the plate. Then remove the central bolt which secures the timing control unit to a taper on the inlet camshaft. Fit a withdrawal bolt (Part No. 024328) in place of the bolt removed, and tighten slightly. Now direct a sharp tap on the end of the withdrawal bolt. This will free the ignition-control unit from the inlet camshaft extension and enable it to be withdrawn.

Do not interfere with the detachable contact-breaker cam which is rotated by two pegs engaged in the plates or the control springs. Should for some reason the cam be removed, note its position prior to removal.

**Correct Ignition-timing Vital.** Incorrect ignition-timing can have a most detrimental effect on the engine, besides reducing its performance. A late timing will result in a "woolly" engine and a hot and noisy exhaust, with considerable overheating and inability to develop full power. An early timing, on the other hand, may result in the engine being powerful on the larger throttle openings, but it will have a nasty tendency to kick-back when being started and it will "knock" readily under slight provocation. Worst of all, the engine will be subjected to some fuel detonation and stresses for which it is *not* designed.

## TIMING THE MAGNETO (1955–7 MODELS)

Never attempt to improve on the maker's timing, which is such that *the contact-breaker contacts begin to open with the piston ½ in. before T.D.C. on the compression stroke.* Sometimes it is necessary for some reason to remove the magneto or its driving chain. Where this is done, the magneto must be retimed. For this purpose it is desirable to have available the following two items—

(*a*) A stout screwdriver, or an old-type tyre lever with the end turned up.
(*b*) A small rod or stout wheel spoke about 5½ in. long.

**1. Before Timing the Magneto.** Remove the covers from (*a*) the contact-breaker, (*b*) the off-side of the rocker-box, and (*c*) the magneto chain-case. Also remove the sparking plug. Check that the gap at the contact-breaker is correct (0·010–0·012 in.) as described on pages 64–66. It is advisable to check that the magneto chain is correctly tensioned. The contact-breaker gap *must* be correct, as this affects the timing appreciably.

Loosen several turns the nut which secures the magneto-driving sprocket to the camshaft, but do not take the nut right off. Then, with the stout screwdriver or old tyre lever referred to above, inserted behind the sprocket, lever the latter off the taper on the camshaft. Rotate the engine forwards slowly until the piston is at true T.D.C. with *both valves closed*, as described below.

**2. Finding Exact Piston Position.** Slip the 5½ in. length of rod through the hole for the sparking plug. Rotate the engine *forwards* slowly until it is felt that the piston is exactly at the top of its stroke. In this position no movement is imparted to the rod. Without moving the piston, mark the rod flush with the top face of the sparking-plug hole. Remove the rod and scratch another mark ½ in. above the first. Again insert the rod through the sparking-plug hole and slowly turn the engine *backwards* by means of the rear wheel (with top gear engaged) until the upper of the two marks on the rod is flush with the top of the sparking plug hole. ½ in. equals 39 deg. before T.D.C.

**3. Timing the Contact "Break."** Turn (with the finger and thumb) *to the maximum extent possible* the front plate of the automatic ignition-control mechanism. This is its fully advanced position. Lock the control in this position by inserting a small wooden wedge. Without moving the piston, rotate the sprocket secured to the magneto armature-shaft (and the driving chain) *anti-clockwise*, viewed from the driving side, until the contacts of the contact-breaker are just beginning to open.

To determine the exact moment of "break," insert a thin Cellophane slip between the contacts and exert a gentle pull on the paper when the magneto sprocket is being slowly turned.

When the exact position of the "break" has been found, secure the sprocket to the camshaft, being most careful not to permit the camshaft and/or armature to move while tightening the camshaft nut.

Finally check over the magneto timing again, verify the chain tension, grease the chain (*see* page 19) if necessary, and replace the covers for the contact-breaker, rocker-box and magneto chain-case. Before replacing the magneto chain-case cover do not forget to remove the wooden wedge previously used to lock the automatic ignition-control mechanism in the fully advanced position. Fit the sparking plug and you should be "all set."

## TIMING THE IGNITION (1958–66)

The maker's recommended ignition timing for 1958 and later coil-ignition models should *never* be altered. *The timing is correct if the contact-breaker contacts begin to open with the piston ½ in. before T.D.C. (top dead centre), with the automatic timing control in the fully advanced position.* Note that the timing is also correct if the contacts begin to open with the piston 8 in. before T.D.C., with the automatic timing-control in the fully *retarded* position. The ignition can therefore be retimed, using one of two methods.

In the event of the automatic timing-control unit being removed from the taper on the inlet camshaft extension, retiming is, of course, necessary. It is also necessary when occasion is had to remove the main cover from the timing case (housing the two camwheels and the engine pinion). The following items are required when retiming the ignition—

(*a*) A small rod or portion of a stiff wheel spoke (about 5½ in. long).

(*b*) An automatic timing-control unit withdrawal tool (Part No. 024328).

Note the following with regard to pre-1964 350 c.c. Model 16 ("Mercury") engines after engine number 41575: the contacts should begin to open with the piston $\frac{11}{32}$ in. before T.D.C. with the automatic timing control fully advanced; on pre-1964 350 c.c. engines after engine number 41575 the contacts should begin to open with the piston $\frac{3}{16}$ in. before T.D.C. when the A.T.C. is fully retarded. On 1964–6 350 and 500 c.c. engines the contacts should begin to open 8·9 mm (34 degrees) and 10·98 mm (38 degrees) before T.D.C. respectively with the automatic timing control fully advanced.

**1. Before Timing the Ignition.** Remove: (*a*) the sparking plug and its h.t. cable; (*b*) the cover from the off-side of the rocker-box; and (*c*) the contact-breaker plate and the automatic timing-control unit. Remove the ignition timing-control unit from the inlet camshaft extension as described on page 68. Before removing the plate, on which the contact-breaker and capacitor are assembled, and behind which the ignition-timing control unit is fitted, check that the contact-breaker gap is correct (*see* page 65). This is important because the gap appreciably affects the ignition timing.

**2. Identifying Piston Position.** Rotate the engine *forwards* slowly until the piston is at or near top dead centre on the compression stroke (inlet valve opens and then closes), with both valves fully closed. Engage fourth gear and insert the timing rod or portion of spoke through the sparking plug hole. Then rock the engine gently backwards and forwards until *no movement* is felt on the rod which should be held as vertically as possible. When the rod remains dead still, with both valves fully closed, the piston is at the extreme top of its stroke, i.e. in the top dead centre (T.D.C.) position.

Scratch a mark on the timing rod flush with the top face of the sparking plug hole, and remove the rod. Then scratch another mark $\frac{1}{2}$ in. or $\frac{1}{8}$ in. *above* the T.D.C. mark, according to whether you decide to retime with the automatic ignition timing-control fully advanced or fully retarded respectively.

**3. Ignition Advance (1955–8 "Magdyno" Models).** On the O.H.V. Norton ES2 the correct ignition timing is $\frac{5}{8}$ in. before T.D.C. on full advance. On Models 19 and 50 the correct ignition timing is $\frac{11}{16}$ in. before T.D.C. with the ignition lever *fully advanced*.

**4. Timing the Ignition.** With the piston at true T.D.C., fit the automatic ignition timing-control unit to the inlet camshaft extension, with the gap formed by the two bob weights (*see* Fig. 33) in line with the two tapped holes for the contact-breaker plate securing screws (shown at 4 in Fig. 34). When correctly positioned the peak of the cam (i.e. its narrowest part) is approximately at 12 o'clock. Press the ignition timing-control unit firmly on to the tapered camshaft extension and deliver a sharp tap on the cam before replacing and tightening the central securing bolt. If the *fully advanced* method of timing is to be used, insert a wooden wedge between the bob weights to fully separate them.

Replace the marked timing rod through the sparking plug hole, and with fourth gear still engaged, turn the engine slowly *backwards* until the *highest* of the two marks scratched on the rod is flush with the top face of the sparking plug hole. Position the contact-breaker plate in its housing (*see* Fig. 34) with the capacitor at 3 o'clock and *lightly* tighten the two screws securing the contact-breaker plate.

To determine the exact moment when the contacts commence to open, insert a thin Cellophane slip between the contacts and exert a gentle pull on the slip when the contact-breaker plate is moved slowly in a *clockwise* direction. When the correct plate position for contact opening is obtained, tighten the two contact-breaker plate securing-screws (if using the fully *retarded* method of ignition timing).

If a wooden wedge is used to *fully advance* the ignition timing, scribe a pencil line on the contact-breaker plate, and a similar line on the plate

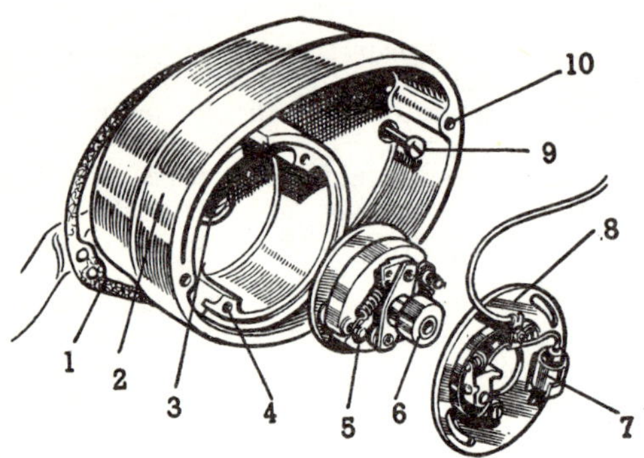


Fig 34 The timing case main cover, automatic ignition timing-control unit and contact-breaker plate shown removed

1. *Washer (between engine timing case and* 2)
2. *Timing-case main cover*
3. *Bush for inlet camshaft extension*
4. *Hole (one of two) for screws securing* 8
5. *Automatic ignition timing-control unit*
6. *Cam (operating contact-breaker)*
7. *Capacitor*
8. *Contact-breaker plate with elongated holes for timing*
9. *Screw (one of five) securing* 2 *to timing case*
10. *Hole (one of two) for screws securing timing-case outer cover*

housing, with both lines in register. Withdraw the contact-breaker plate, remove the wedge, replace the contact-breaker plate with the two scribed lines in register. Afterwards fully tighten the two contact-breaker plate securing-screws. Before replacing the sparking plug, h.t. lead, and rocker-box cover, again check the ignition timing.

## ADJUSTING THE TAPPETS

This is another routine maintenance operation, and a very important one. Check and, if necessary, rectify the tappet adjustment every 3000 miles. It is generally necessary to adjust both tappets after every 5000 miles. The adjustment must always be checked after decarbonizing the engine and grinding-in the valves. The need for tappet adjustment more frequently than about once very 5000 miles is generally due to some fault which should be investigated. It is of vital importance to keep the adjustment correct in order to prevent damage to the valves and to maintain high engine performance.

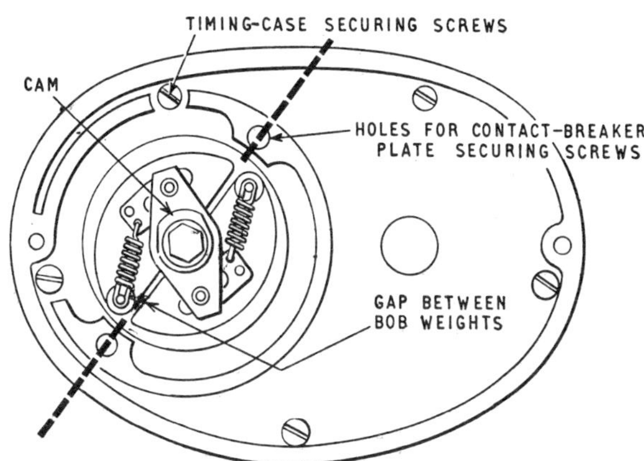


Fig 35 Correct alignment when fitting the automatic ignition timing-control unit

*Note the cam position and the dotted alignment line.*

**The Adjustment.** On 350, 500 c.c. models the correct tappet clearance is *nil* with both valves closed and the engine *cold* (warm, not hot, on all 1955–66 models). A clearance of *nil* implies that the push-rods are free to rotate without any appreciable up-and-down play.

Detach the cover from the off side of the rocker-box after removing the three retaining nuts and fibre washers. This exposes the inlet and exhaust tappet adjustment. As may be seen in Fig. 36, each push-rod has an adjustable head *A* secured by a lock-nut *B* to the push-rod sleeve *C*. First see that the valve lifter has some backlash.

Note that a new sleeve cannot be fitted to an existing light-alloy push-rod, the sleeve and the rod being simultaneously threaded (internally) for the adjustable head, during manufacture.

**Adjusting the Tappets (All 1955–66 Engines).** Turn the engine (350 c.c. or 500 c.c.) over slowly until the piston is at T.D.C. on the compression stroke, with both valves closed. See that the exhaust-valve lifter is not preventing the exhaust valve from seating fully. Then check the tappet clearance for both tappets (*see* above). Referring to Fig. 36, if an adjustment of either or both tappets is required, hold the push-rod sleeve *C* with one spanner, and with another loosen the lock-nut *B*. Then screw the adjustable head *A* up or down until a tappet clearance of *nil* is obtained. Afterwards tighten the lock-nut *B* (without moving head *A*) and again check the clearance.

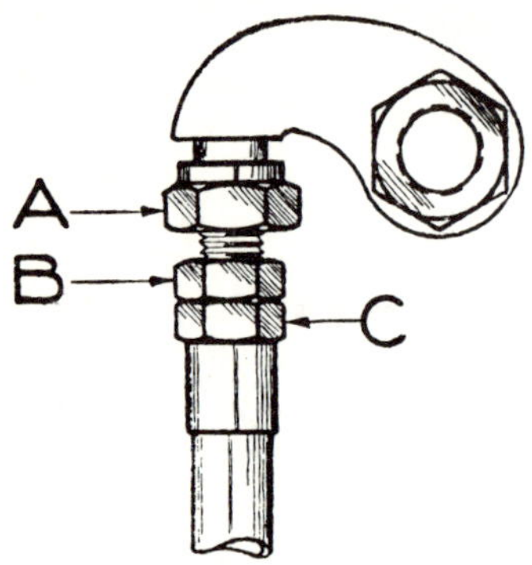


Fig 36 Tappet adjustment on all 1955–66 O.H.V. engines including Norton

**After a Tappet Adjustment.** Turn the engine over until both valves are closed. Check that the push-rods are free to rotate without appreciable up-and-down movement. Fit the cover to the off-side of the rocker-box and replace the three retaining nuts. Make sure that the three fibre washers are also replaced beneath the nuts. When tightening the nuts, avoid using excessive pressure on the spanner. Such pressure is quite unnecessary, because a rubber fillet is incorporated at the rocker-box cover joint. Moderate pressure with the spanner will suffice to prevent oil leakage. Tighten the three nuts evenly.

## DECARBONIZING AND VALVE GRINDING

The exact time at which the removal of carbon deposits becomes necessary depends to some extent on (*a*) quality of the fuel used and (*b*) the driving conditions. Under normal circumstances it is advisable to remove the cylinder head, decarbonize and, *if necessary*, grind-in the valves *when* the performance declines. If the engine develops a tendency to "knock" when accelerating quickly or hill-climbing, has a reduced general performance, and heavy petrol consumption, this indicates that the time for decarbonizing is due.

Do *not* remove the cylinder barrel unless you have *good* reason to inspect the piston and rings, and perhaps the bore of the cylinder. Remove the barrel, however, if any stiffness of the piston occurs, or if loss of compression (not caused by bad valve seating) develops. Decarbonizing and grinding-in the valves are quite simple if you follow the correct procedure (sections 1—22).

**1. Remove Fuel Tank.** It is necessary to remove the fuel tank before detaching the rocker-box and cylinder head prior to decarbonizing, also when undertaking any major engine overhaul work.

To remove the petrol tank on 1955–9 models first close both petrol taps and remove the cap nut which secures each petrol pipe banjo connector. Use one spanner to hold the tap and another spanner to unscrew the cap nut. Be careful not to lose the four fibre washers, fitted one on each side of each banjo connection. Sever the wires which interlace the four tank-fixing bolts. Then remove the bolts and withdraw the tank. Note the layout (*see* Fig. 41) of the various rubber and metal washers and tubular sleeves to ensure correct replacement.

To remove the petrol tank of 1960–1 models first turn off the petrol and disconnect both petrol pipes, release the dualseat front fixing bolts, and raise the dualseat slightly. Now remove the two fixing bolts securing the front end of the tank (*see* Fig. 41) and also remove the rear fixing bolt. Then remove the petrol tank.

To remove the petrol tank on 1962–6 models first turn off the petrol and disconnect both petrol pipes. The tank is secured by two nuts at the front end and also by a rubber ring encircling the frame tube and anchored on two tank projections. A rubber block is provided between the bottom of the tank and the frame tube. Remove the two nuts on each of the two front tank-mountings. Then depress or pull back the "nose" of the dualseat, lift off the rubber band from its anchorage, and withdraw the tank.

**2. Remove Rocker-box (1955–66).** After tank removal, the next step towards cylinder-head removal is to take off the rocker-box and push-rods. First remove the three nuts retaining the cover to the off side of the rocker-box. Also remove the three fibre washers beneath the nuts. Then take off the rocker-box cover. Disconnect the upper union of the oil-feed pipe from the pump to the rocker-box. Now rotate the engine slowly until both inlet and exhaust valves are closed. Detach the engine-steady bracket (*see* Fig. 37) between the engine and frame by removing the nuts and washers from the rocker-box bolt extensions and also the bolt from the frame clip.

With a spanner, remove the nine bolts securing the rocker-box to the cylinder head. Disconnect the exhaust-valve-lifter cable. Grip the rocker-box, tilt up its right-hand side and withdraw both push-rods. These should not be interchanged, and for this reason should be marked or placed so that they can subsequently be identified. Now carefully lift the rocker-box clear of the cylinder head.

**3. Remove Cylinder Head.** Having removed the fuel tank and rocker-box as previously described, unscrew the sparking plug.

Should the sparking plug be difficult to unscrew, do not apply excessive

Fig 37 Preparing for rocker-box removal

*The petrol tank, the oil-feed pipe to the rocker-box, and the rocker-box cover have been removed. The next operation is to remove the engine-steady bracket connecting the rocker-box to the frame top-tube, and then remove the rocker-box securing bolts.*

force with the box spanner. Brush some paraffin around the plug body and allow to soak prior to further use of the spanner.

Then proceed to remove, or partially remove, the exhaust system.

To remove the exhaust system, first remove the nuts and washers which secure the exhaust pipe and silencer to their stays. Then pull the exhaust pipe and silencer away from the stays, and pull the pipe downwards from the port in the cylinder head.

Remove the Amal carburettor by disconnecting the air filter (where fitted) and removing the two nuts securing the carburettor flange to the cylinder head. The carburettor may be allowed to rest on the saddle or on the platform above the dynamo (1955–7); it is not necessary to remove the throttle and air slides from the carburettor.

Next remove the four bolts which retain the cylinder head to the cylinder barrel. If these are stiff, brush paraffin round their heads and allow to penetrate before again using the spanner. Lift the cylinder head from the cylinder barrel and simultaneously remove the push-rod cover tubes which come away with the cylinder head.

**4. To Remove Cylinder Barrel.** Rotate the engine so that the piston is near B.D.C. Next remove the four nuts which secure the cylinder barrel to the crankcase, and then gently draw the barrel off the piston. Steady the latter with one hand as the barrel is withdrawn, and take great care not to allow the piston to fall sharply against the connecting-rod. After removing the cylinder barrel, cover the mouth of the crankcase with a clean rag.

**5. Removing Piston.** To remove the fully-floating gudgeon-pin, it is only necessary to extract *one* circlip with the special pliers provided in tool kit. Push the gudgeon-pin out from the opposite side and remove the piston. The gudgeon-pin is an easy sliding fit in the piston bosses and the small-end bush. If the piston is not of the split-skirt type, scratch an "F" on the inside to indicate which is the front. Mark the pin also.

*Piston Condition.* A piston will run well for many thousands of miles; but eventually loss of compression and/or piston slap occurs due to wear of the piston, rings, and cylinder bore, especially the last-mentioned. Examine the cylinder bore occasionally for longitudinal scores and circumferential ridges. Also inspect the piston for blackening of the skirt, scores, smearing, and other possible damage, particularly near the ring lands.

*Rebores.* After a very considerable mileage (when wear at the top of the bore reaches 0·008 in.) it is usually essential to have a rebore and fit an oversize piston and rings to restore the compression and performance of the engine to normal. The makers provide for rebores 0·020 in. and 0·040 in. oversize, and can supply 0·020 in. and 0·040 in. oversize pistons and rings to suit. Running-in is, of course, necessary after a rebore.

**6. Piston Ring Removal.** The piston rings should not be disturbed if their condition is good, they are free in their grooves, and engine compression remains good. The rings can be removed by "peeling off" with a small knife, but it is preferable to remove them with the aid of three strips of thin sheet metal (about ¼ in. wide) inserted beneath each ring as shown in Fig. 38. The rings, being made of cast iron, cannot safely be sprung out wider than the piston-crown diameter. If the rings are stuck with carbon, apply some paraffin. If this fails, use a proprietary ring removal tool.

**7. Inspecting Piston Rings.** Inspect the two compression rings and the scraper ring very carefully. To ensure good engine-compression the piston rings must have good springiness, be free, but not slack in their grooves, have a polished surface all round, and have their gaps equally spaced and

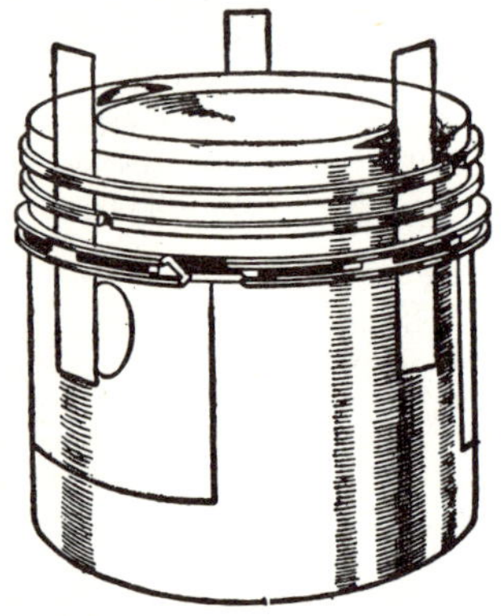

Fig 38 The safest method of removing and fitting piston rings

of the correct size. If inspection reveals that the ring surfaces are bright all round, they are obviously making good circumferential contact with the cylinder bore and can be regarded as serviceable. If, on the other hand, the surfaces are discoloured or scorched at some points, contact is poor and it is desirable to reject the rings and fit new ones. The same applies where the rings are vertically slack in their grooves.

Clean the rings thoroughly on their inside faces, also the ends of the rings, and the slots in the scraper ring (*see* Fig. 38). Piston rings are made to very precise dimensions, and it is not generally practicable to fit over-size rings unless the piston is renewed also. Always fit genuine factory rings which are dimensionally correct. To reduce cylinder bore wear, a chromium-plated top compression ring is fitted to 1955 and later 350 and 500 c.c. engines.

**8. Piston Ring Dimensions.** The widths of the compression rings and the slotted scraper-ring on all engines are $\frac{1}{16}$ in. and ⅛ in. respectively. The normal ring gap is 0·006 in. and rings should be renewed when the gap exceeds 0·030 in. The normal clearance of each ring in its groove is 0·003 in. (0·002 in. on 1955–65 engines). Norton ring gaps are 0·012 in.

After a considerable mileage, or if loss of compression occurs with the valves in good condition, check the gap of each piston ring. The best method of checking the gap is to push the ring squarely into the bore of the cylinder barrel with the aid of the piston and then check the gap between the ends of the ring with a feeler gauge. If the gap proves excessive, fit correct new rings already "gapped" to 0·006 in.

**9. To Remove Valves (1955 Onwards).** On 1955 and later engines a modified and improved hairpin valve-spring assembly renders it unnecessary to employ a valve-spring compressor to remove the valves, though a compressor (*see* Fig. 40) is needed for replacing them. To remove each hairpin valve-spring, insert a finger in the spring coil and pull the coil sharply upward. You can then take off the valve-spring collar and split collet, and withdraw the valve. If the tapered split collet is stuck, deliver a sharp tap on the collar to free it.

Note that the modified seat for the valve-spring has a raised impression on its under side; this registers with a hole drilled in the valve-guide boss to ensure proper location. Note also that, as hitherto, the valves are not interchangeable and must be identified for correct replacement.

**10. Scraping Off the Carbon.** The best tool to use for scraping off the carbon deposits is an old (blunted) screwdriver, or a proprietary scraper (obtainable from most accessory dealers). For cleaning piston-ring grooves a suitable scraper can be made up by fitting a handle to a piece of broken piston-ring, or better still a proprietary tool can be obtained for the purpose. It is worth while decarbonizing *thoroughly*, as carbon deposits form less rapidly on smooth surfaces. Where head deposits are found to be very hard, some paraffin will facilitate their removal.

If the cylinder barrel has not been removed, scrape off all carbon from the piston crown, but *on no account use any abrasive*. Should this get between the piston and cylinder (as it probably would) your machine would rapidly go into a decline! Be very careful not to make any deep scratch marks on the comparatively soft surface of the light-alloy piston. Scrape off all carbon from the inside of the combustion chamber. Do not forget to chip off and completely remove all carbon from the valve ports, the vicinity of the valves, the valve heads, and the sparking-plug hole. If close inspection reveals any roughness of the metal surfaces inside the inlet or exhaust port, it is beneficial to smooth out such irregularities with a curved riffler. It is permissible to use some *fine* emery-cloth to polish up a cast iron combustion chamber surface, but if this is done the cylinder head must afterwards be very thoroughly cleaned and all trace of abrasive particles removed. Use a rag damped with paraffin. Do not touch the cylinder bore.

If the cylinder barrel *and* piston have been removed, it may be advisable to scrape carbon off the inside of the piston, but unless the deposits are thick, this should not be done. Remove all carbon from the piston crown, but *do not touch the skirt*. Any attempt to scrape the piston skirt may have disastrous results. The piston-ring grooves sometimes need attention. Clean these up thoroughly, but be very careful not to damage

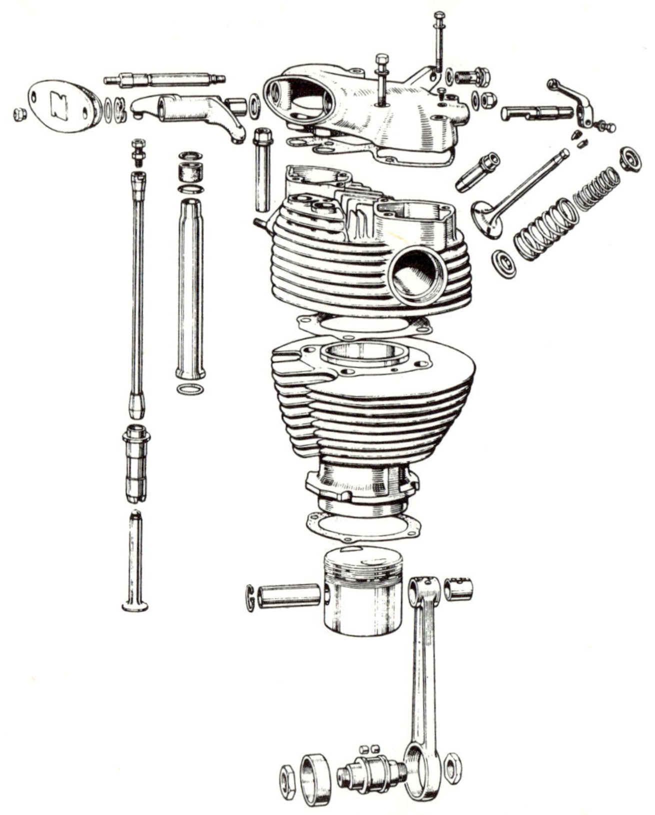

Fig 39 Exploded view of 1957–62 Norton engine Models 19, ES2, 50

the actual metal comprising the sides of the grooves. Make sure that the holes in the groove for the scraper ring (*see* Fig. 38) are unobstructed. The cleaning of piston rings is referred to on page 78. After decarbonizing is complete, clean all parts thoroughly with suitable clean rags and paraffin.

**11. How to Grind-in the Valves.** Although the engine manufacturers recommend that the valves be inspected every time the engine is decarbonized, it should be understood that excessive valve grinding is not advisable as this is liable to cause the valves to become "pocketed," with a resultant loss of engine efficiency.

To grind-in a valve, first smear the bevelled face of the valve with a *thin* layer of grinding paste. If the valve face and seat are only slightly pitted, it should be sufficient to use a *fine* grade of paste only. Serious pitting may necessitate the preliminary application of a coarse grade, and if the pitting is very severe, it may be necessary to have the valve seats refaced at a garage with a cutter.

Insert the valve in its seat and oscillate the valve about a quarter of a turn backwards and forwards by means of a suitable valve holder. Maintain a slight pressure between the valve and its seat and lift the valve occasionally (when the abrasive ceases to bite) and turn it to a new position. Continue to grind-in the valve until a continuous matt ring is present on both the valve seat and the valve. Generally one application of grinding paste is sufficient for the inlet valve, but the exhaust valve may require several applications to obtain good results.

**12. After Grinding-in Valves.** See that every trace of grinding paste is eradicated by cleaning the valves and the two seats with petrol and a clean rag. To ensure that the valve guides are free from damaging abrasive, it is advisable to draw a piece of clean rag moistened with petrol through both guides.

**13. To check Valve-spring Length (1955–66).** After much use the hard-pressed valve-springs may weaken under the influence of heat, and thereby spoil the quick and positive action of the valves, which is so vital to high engine-efficiency. The condition of the valve springs is reflected in their free length, which should be checked very occasionally with a small rule.

All 1955–65 A.J.S./Matchless O.H.V. engines have hairpin instead of coil-type valve-springs. Renew any hairpin valve spring whose free length is $\frac{3}{16}$–$\frac{1}{4}$ in. less than its normal free length: 2 in. (between the centre of wire).

**Changing Valve Guides.** To remove an inlet valve guide, clean thoroughly the protruding end of the guide. Then apply some gentle heat and press the guide downwards. To remove an exhaust valve guide, apply some gentle heat, press the guide upwards enough to allow removal of the external circlip. Afterwards clean the top of the guide, and remove by pressing downwards. When replacing a valve guide, apply some gentle heat, press in, and see that the guide projects ½ in. Make sure that the oil hole in the guide is correctly aligned.

**14. To Replace Valves (1955 Onwards).** Thoroughly clean the bores of both valve guides and smear a film of engine oil on the stems of the valves. Replace the latter in their correct guides. On 350 c.c. engines the inlet valve can be immediately identified as it has a head of larger diameter than the exhaust valve-head. On 500 c.c. engines, however, the dimension of both valves are identical though the material used differs. In this case, before fitting the valves, note the markings "IN" and "EX" on top of the inlet and exhaust-valve stems respectively. These are above the grooves for the split collets. Insert suitable packing beneath each valve head and place the cylinder head in its normal position on the bench. Then fit each hairpin valve-spring as described below.

Fit the valve-spring top collar and the split collet. Make quite sure that the two machined grooves on the bore of the split collet register with the corresponding rings on the valve stem. Then position the hairpin valve-springs and proceed to compress each spring with the special valve-spring compressor shown in Fig. 40. The standard tool kit does not include this compressor, but it can be obtained from the makers or a motor-cycle dealer. To use the compressor, apply the upper end of the valve-spring to the groove in the top cap; insert a short rod (e.g. a rocker-box securing bolt) through the holes in the compressor (and the valve-spring coils) and pull upward and outward until the end of the spring prong can be rested on the seat. Then with the finger, press down.

Remove the rod (or rocker-box bolt) as soon as the compressor lies against the cylinder head, but maintain finger pressure until you have removed the rod (or bolt) and also the compressor tool. Finally push the spring down until it locates properly. Its prong ends must lie flat on the seat.

**15. Replacing Piston Rings.** If these have been removed, fit them in their grooves, which should be oiled. The safest method of fitting the piston rings is to use three strips of thin sheet metal, as illustrated in Fig. 38. Fit the (bottom) scraper ring first, and then the two compression rings. Space the ring gaps evenly, that is, at 120 degrees to each other. It is assumed that the ring gaps are within the permissible limits (*see* page 78). If new rings are fitted, these are correctly "gapped" by the makers and are ready for immediate use.

On 1955 and many subsequent O.H.V. engines the top compression ring is chromium plated and one edge is marked TOP. See that this ring is replaced accordingly. Note that after a considerable mileage the word TOP may become unreadable, but for a very considerable period the correct assembly position for the chromium-plated ring can be determined by the extra brightness of the edge which makes contact with the cylinder

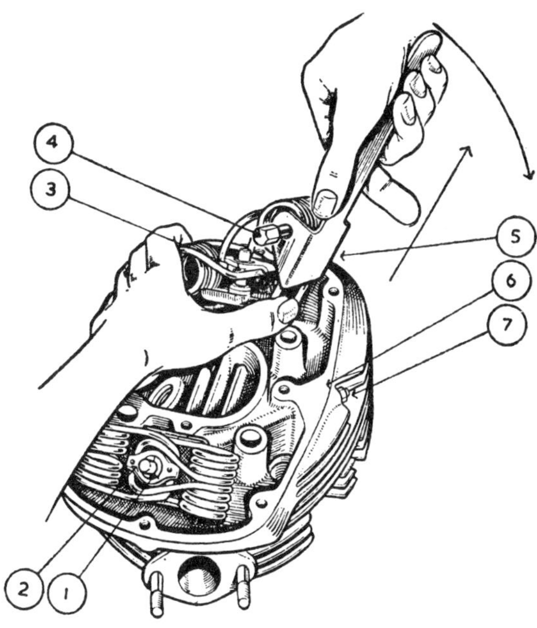


Fig 40 Valve-spring compressor (Part No. 018276) for engines with hairpin valve-springs (1955 onwards)

1. *Split collet*
2. *Valve-spring collar*
3. *Valve-spring collar*
4. *Rocker-box bolt*
5. *Valve-spring compressor*
6. *Oil duct from rocker-box to inlet-valve guide*
7. *Screw controlling oil feed to inlet-valve stem*

bore. The bright edge must be at the *bottom*. When eventually the ring becomes bright over its full width (indicating full contact with the bore), it is permissible to replace the top compression ring either way round.

**16. Replacing Piston.** It is assumed that all parts are thoroughly clean and that the piston rings have been refitted. Smear some engine oil on the gudgeon-pin and then offer up the piston to the small-end of the connecting-rod. The piston must be replaced in *exactly* the same position as before. If it is of the split-skirt type the split itself must face to the *front* of the machine. This is essential.

Next insert the gudgeon-pin from the side from which the circlip has been removed. Centralize the gudgeon-pin, and with the snip-nose pliers in the tool kit, replace the circlip, using a rotary movement to ensure that it beds snugly into its groove. Perfect fitting of the circlip is essential to prevent damage. If the condition of the old circlip is suspect, renew the circlip immediately.

**17. To Replace Cylinder Barrel.** A *new* washer must be fitted to the crankcase and its cylinder barrel side should be coated with liquid jointing-compound. Make sure that none of the compound chokes any of the oil holes and that the holes register properly. Now smear some engine oil on the piston and cylinder bore, and then turn the engine so that the piston is at or near B.D.C. Verify that the piston-ring gaps are spaced at 120 degrees and remove the rag from the mouth of the crankcase.

Ease the cylinder barrel carefully over the piston, carefully compressing each ring as it enters the bore mouth, to enable the barrel to slide over the piston without friction. Finally replace the four cylinder-barrel retaining nuts. Tighten the four nuts, first finger-tight, and then firmly in a diagonal order, turning each nut about one-quarter of a turn at a time.

**18. Fit the Cylinder Head.** Wipe the bottom face of the cylinder head and the top edge of the cylinder barrel absolutely clean. Then fit the push-rod cover tubes to the cylinder head. See that the rubber gaskets are in good condition, and fitted between the top ends of the cover tubes and cylinder head. If the push-rod cover tubes were pulled away from the cylinder head during stripping down, it will probably be found that the rubber gaskets have remained located in the cylinder head. Also check that the metal washers are interposed between the top edges of the rubber gaskets and the recesses in the cylinder head.

Fit the cylinder-head gasket on the top edge of the cylinder barrel. If the gasket is not in perfect condition, renew it. Whether you fit a new gasket or use the old one, it is advisable to anneal it just before placing it on the cylinder barrel. To anneal the gasket, heat it to a "blood red" colour and plunge into cold clean water. Place the two rubber glands round the inlet and exhaust tappet guides. Then replace the cylinder head on the barrel, complete with push-rod cover tubes, and fit the four cylinder head retaining bolts. Each bolt must be fitted with a plain steel washer. Tighten each bolt a few turns and then gradually tighten all four, using a diagonal sequence to ensure an even pressure being exerted on the cylinder head.

**19. Fit Rocker-box (1955 Onwards).** Clean the lower face of the rocker-box and the upper face of the cylinder head. Next slowly turn the engine until the piston is at T.D.C. with both tappets right down. Inspect the cylinder-head composition washer (renew if not perfect), and lay the washer on the cylinder head.

Position the rocker-box and then raise slightly the off side of the box to permit of the two long push-rods being inserted in their original positions. Now fit the *nine* rocker-box securing bolts. Note that the bolt with the short head goes in the centre right-hand position, while the bolts having the threaded extensions go one on each side of the central short-headed bolt. Tighten in a diagonal order and evenly all nine rocker-box securing bolts.

Next fit the engine steady stay and then rotate the engine a few times so as to be sure that the various parts bed right down. Now reconnect the exhaust-valve lifter control and check the tappet clearances.

**20. Fit Pipe and Cover.** Reconnect the oil-feed pipe from the pump to the rocker-box. 1964–6 models have a by-pass from the main oil feed, taken from the timing-case cover. Use two spanners when tightening the upper union, to prevent the union (screwed into the rocker-box) from turning. Fit a new rubber fillet to the rocker-box side cover if examination of the fillet shows deterioration. Then fit the rocker-box side cover to the rocker-box, and replace the three fibre washers and securing nuts. Tighten these nuts evenly, but not too tightly. The provision of a rubber fillet renders excessive tightening quite unnecessary.

**21. Final Engine Assembly.** Final reassembly, after decarbonizing, is completed by replacing the Amal carburettor, the sparking plug, exhaust system. When fitting the Amal carburettor, it is important to obtain an absolutely air-tight joint at the attachment flange. Renew the washer if not perfect, also the copper washer for the sparking plug. Smear some graphite paste on the plug threads.

**22. Replace Fuel Tank (1955–9).** The arrangement of the fuel tank-fixing bolts and washers on 1955–9 motor-cycles is shown in Fig. 41. As may be seen, an identical arrangement is provided for each of the four mounting brackets. Metal sleeves (shown at *E*) are included to enable the fixing bolts to be *fully* tightened without over compressing the rubber pads. To replace the petrol tank, proceed as follows—

1. Insert one of the four sleeves (*E*) in each of the four thick rubber pads (*B*), so that the top of the sleeve is flush with the top of the pad.
2. Lay the four thick rubber pads (*B*) on the ends of the four petrol tank support-brackets, complete with sleeves (*E*) protruding through the bracket holes.
3. Correctly position the fuel tank.

4. Slide one of the four metal washers (*A*) over each of the four tank-fixing bolts (*D*). Afterwards slip a thin rubber pad (*C*) over each tank-fixing bolt.

5. Insert all four tank-fixing bolts, complete with rubber pads and metal washers.

6. Tighten *firmly* the four tank-fixing bolts.

7. Interlace the four tank-fixing bolts in pairs, using 22 gauge copper wire.

8. Reconnect both petrol pipes, and with a spanner hold the taps when firmly tightening the cap-nuts.

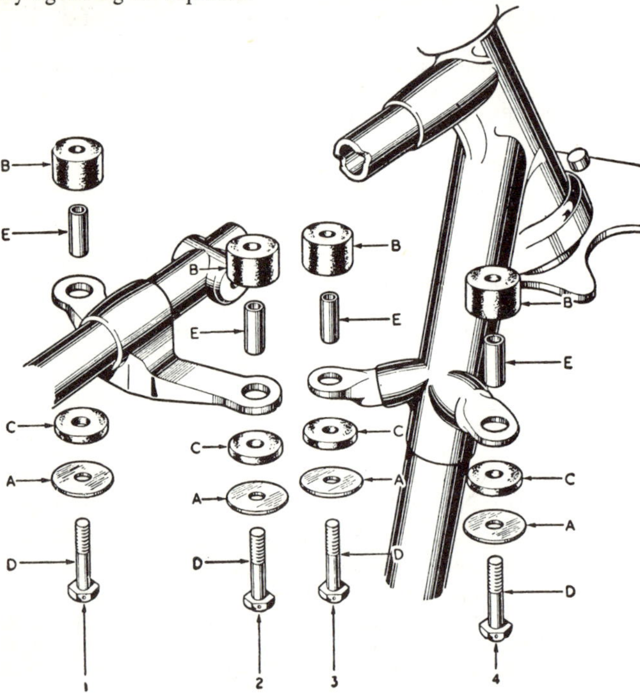


Fig 41 Fuel-tank mounting (1955–9)

*With the arrangement shown, which includes four sleeves, the tank-fixing bolts can and must be fully tightened on assembly. On 1960–1 models two bolts secure the front of the tank, and one bolt the rear.*

*A. Metal washer*
*B. Thick rubber pad*
*C. Thin rubber pad*
*D. Petrol tank-fixing bolt*
*E. Metal sleeve for fixing bolt D*

**Replacing Fuel Tank (1960–1).** The method of securing the petrol tank is similar to that used on 1955–9 models and shown in Fig. 41 except that *three* instead of four fixing bolts are used, two at the front and one at the rear. The rubber pads, washers and sleeves are similar and similarly arranged. The 1955–9 instructions therefore apply except in regard to the number of fixing bolt assemblies to be fitted.

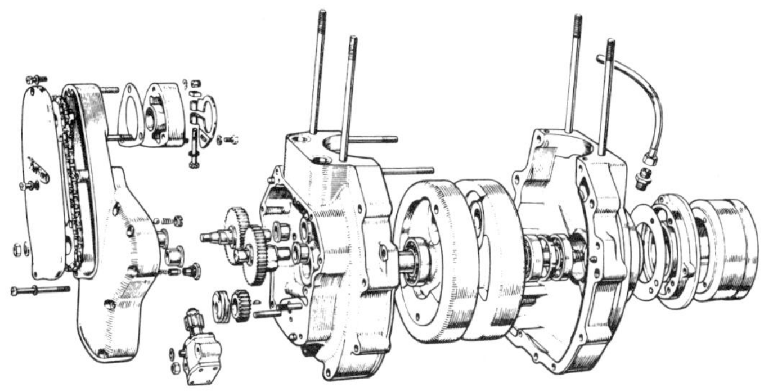

Fig 42 Lower part of Norton engine 1959–62

**Replacing Fuel Tank (1962–6 Models).** The replacement of the fuel tank is quite straightforward. See that the rubber block at the rear of the frame tube is properly located. Position the fuel tank and anchor the rubber ring, which encircles the frame tube, to the projections on the fuel tank. Tighten securely the two front fixing nuts. Finally reconnect the two petrol pipes and push forward the "nose" of the dualseat.

**To Dismantle Timing Gears (1955–7).** First remove the foot gear-change pedal to render accessible the timing case. Then remove the cover from the magneto chain-case by unscrewing the six securing screws. Also remove the rocker-box cover after removing the three fixing nuts and fibre washers Slacken the magneto driving-chain if it is tight.

Unscrew the nut (R.H. thread) that secures the sprocket to the magneto armature spindle and remove this nut and the washer behind it. With a suitable tool, lever the sprocket off the spindle taper. Should the sprocket be stiff, use a suitable sprocket-drawer. Remove the magneto driving-chain and withdraw the sprocket from the camshaft in the same manner employed to withdraw the other sprocket. The securing nut for this sprocket also has a R.H. thread. Next turn the engine so that *both valves are closed*.

With a screwdriver, remove the five screws that secure the combined magneto chain-case and timing cover to the timing-case. The timing gear is then exposed. Before completely removing the timing-case cover, hold the two camwheels in position in case they should come adrift when the cover is lifted clear. The two camwheels may then be removed by pulling the camshafts from their bearings.

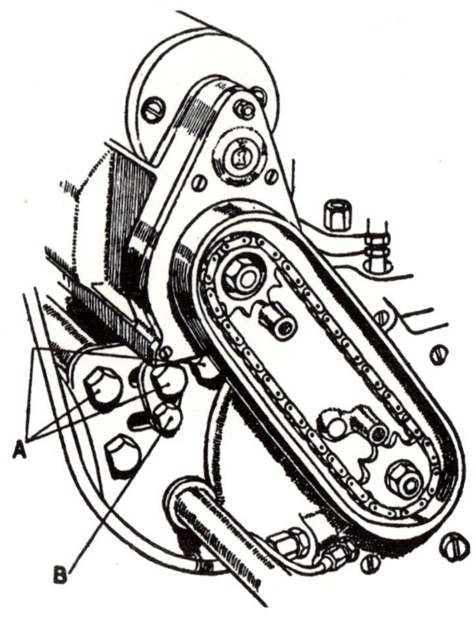


Fig 43 Norton "Magdyno" securing bolts *A*(3) and locking bolt *B*, also chain and driving sprockets

Generally it is unnecessary to remove the small engine pinion, but if for some reason you decide to extract the pinion, you should undo the nut (L.H. thread) and with a suitable extractor pull the pinion off the crankshaft taper to which it is keyed (one key). To assemble the timing gears, use the procedure for dismantling in the reverse order.

**To Dismantle Timing Gears (1958–66).** Remove the foot gear-change pedal and then remove the outer cover from the timing case after removing its two securing screws. Next remove the contact-breaker plate and the automatic ignition-control unit as described on page 68. Then remove the five screws which retain the timing-case main cover (*see* Fig. 34) and pull away the cover. This exposes the twin-camwheel timing gear shown in Fig. 45. If the washer (shown at 1 in Fig. 34) is damaged, this must be renewed. While removing the timing-case main cover, hold both camwheels in position in case they should come away during the withdrawal of the cover. Now pull the inlet and exhaust camshafts from their bearings.

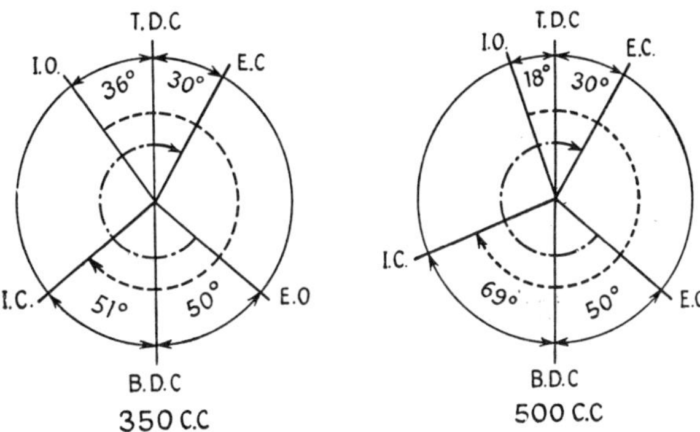


Fig 44 Valve timing diagrams (1955–65 engines)

*The above timings assume the valves to be* 0·001 *in. off their seats. When checking the valve timing on all engines, set both tappet clearances at* 0·016 *in. to ensure that the tappets are well clear of the quietening curves.*

The small engine pinion is a taper fit and is keyed on to the timing-side shaft. The mark on the pinion is central with the keyway. Removal of the pinion is rarely required. To remove the pinion undo the retaining nut (left-hand thread) and with a suitable extractor pull the pinion off the tapered timing-side shaft. Use the dismantling procedure in the reverse order for assembling, and re-time the ignition (*see* page 70).

**When Fitting Timing Cover (1964–6 Engines).** On 1964–5 engines with a gear-type pump it is important to see that the oil seal is under light pressure when fitting the timing cover. The pressure of the oil seal should move the timing cover outwards, making a gap of about 0·010 in. If no pressure exists, fit packing shims between the oil seal and the pump body. Excessive pressure should be avoided as this can mutilate the oil seal and cause leakage.

**Retiming the Valves (1955–66).** To ensure that the valve timing is correct, it is necessary to use the following procedure when assembling the timing gears—

1. Turn the engine slowly until the dot mark on the small engine pinion is in line with the centre of the bush for the inlet camshaft. The bush concerned is the *rear* one.

2. Fit the inlet camshaft so that the dot mark on the camwheel registers with the dot mark on the small engine pinion.

3. Turn the engine slowly *forward* until the dot mark on the small engine pinion is in line with the centre of the bush for the exhaust camshaft (the front bush).

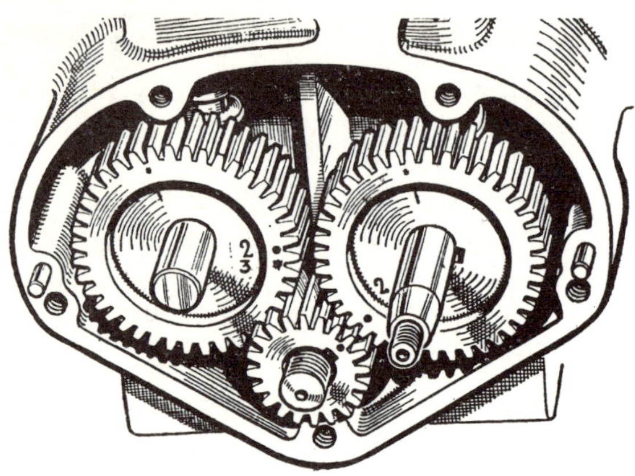


Fig 45 The (1955–7) twin camwheel timing gear with 1955 dot system of timing marks

*Note the following: the nut securing the small engine pinion (which has one dot) is shown removed: the inlet camshaft shown has no tapered extension which is provided on 1958–66 coil-ignition models to secure the automatic ignition-control unit.*

4. Fit the exhaust camshaft so that the dot mark on the cam-wheel registers with the dot mark on the engine pinion.

If both camwheels are aligned in accordance with the above procedure, the valve timing *must* be correct, provided the timing-gear teeth have not become excessively worn, in which case it is time that the engine and machine are completely overhauled. It is advisable after assembling the timing gears to check that the tappet adjustment (*see* page 72) is correct, as this affects the valve timing to a small extent. Also check the magneto-chain tension (*see* page 67) and magneto timing on 1955–7 engines.

**On 1955 Engines.** The inlet camwheel has *three* timing dots marked 1, 2, 3; the exhaust camwheel has two dots marked 1 and 2 as shown in Fig. 45.

On 350 c.c. touring engines align the dot marked 3 on the inlet camwheel with the single dot on the engine pinion. On 500 c.c. touring engines align the timing dot marked 2 on the inlet camwheel with the dot on the engine pinion. The dot marked 2 must also always be used for the exhaust camwheel on all 1955 350 c.c. and 500 c.c. engines.

**On 1956–66 Engines.** After replacing the timing case-cover on coil-ignition models the ignition must be re-timed (*see* page 70) when fitting the automatic ignition-control unit and the contact-breaker plate.

When fitting the inlet camwheel on 1956–63 350 c.c. and 500 c.c. engines align the dot marked 3 or 2 respectively with the dot mark on the engine pinion. When fitting the exhaust camwheel, align the dot marked 1 with the dot on the engine pinion, and disregard dots marked 2, 3 (*see* Fig. 45). 1964–6 camwheels have a single dot mark.

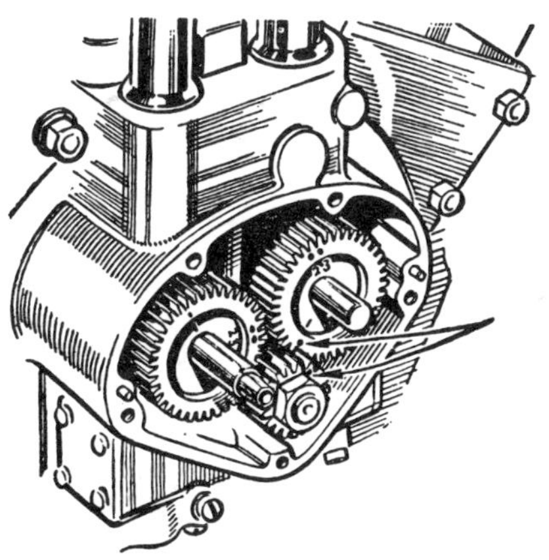

Fig 46 The 1958–66 twin camwheel timing gear with 1956–63 dot system of timing marks

*Note that on all Matchless engines the dot mark on the inlet camwheel must always be aligned with the dot on the engine pinion before the exhaust camwheel is dealt with. The arrows show the exhaust camwheel dot marked 1 aligned with the engine pinion dot. The camwheels on all 1964–5 engines have only one dot.*

**Checking by Degree Method.** If for any reason you make an actual check on the valve timing by attaching a degree disc to the crankshaft, it is essential *before* starting to check the timing to adjust both tappet clearances to 0·016 in. with the piston at T.D.C. on the compression stroke. A degree disc (Part No. 022011) is available.

## MAINTENANCE OF MOTOR-CYCLE PARTS

Although engine maintenance is vital, do not neglect the tyres and the lighting system, and pay due regard to the correct lubrication and adjustment of the motor-cycle parts.

**Items Necessary for Maintenance.** It is desirable to have the following items available: a can of paraffin, a stiff brush, a tin of *summer grade* engine oil, a canister of light grease (*see* page 23), a tin of hydraulic fluid and a flask graduated in fluid oz. (*see* page 26), a tyre pressure gauge, a Lucas hydrometer and battery filler, a tyre repair outfit, and a receptacle for draining the gearbox and oil-bath chain case.

For cleaning purposes the following are also needed: some jars or a pail, some non-fluffy rags, two chamois leathers, a sponge and pail (if no hose is available), some soft dusters, and a tin of polish for the enamelled parts.

**Tools Required.** The basic tool kit is sufficient for all routine maintenance, stripping down and assembly, but it is desirable to buy a chain-rivet extractor and a box of spare chain links. If you are in the mood to tackle repair work as well as maintenance, consider the various Matchless service tools available.

**The Lighting System.** Keep the lights bright by attending to lamp, battery, and dynamo maintenance as described in Chapter 4.

**Lubrication of Cycle Parts.** This is fully explained in Chapter 2. Attend to the lubrication points indicated at 5 to 17 in the Lubrication Chart on page 21.

**Keep the Machine Clean.** If the enamelled and chromium-plated parts are neglected, the machine will soon become shabby-looking, and serious rusting may occur. On no account leave your machine soaking wet overnight. If you have not time for thorough cleaning in wet weather, grease the machine all over before using it. When cleaning the machine, use a stiff brush and paraffin for removing filth from the lower parts.

**Cleaning Enamelled Parts.** Never try to remove caked mud by attempting to brush or rub it off when dry. Instead, cautiously soak it off by means of a hose. When doing this, be careful not to direct the stream of water on to vital and vulnerable components such as the carburettor, dynamo, and magneto. If no hose is available, soak off the mud with a pail of water and a sponge. After removing all mud and dirt, dry the enamelled parts with a chamois leather, and afterwards polish the surfaces with soft dusters and a proprietary polish.

**How to Clean Chromium.** On no account use ordinary liquid metal polish or paste to clean any of the chromium-plated parts. Such cleaners generally contain oleic acid which attacks the chromium. It is permissible, however, to clean the surfaces occasionally with some special chromium cleaning compound. To remove tarnish (salt deposits), it is advisable to clean the surfaces regularly with a damp chamois leather and afterwards polish them with a soft duster.

**During Winter.** It is a good plan to apply with a soft cloth to all chromium-plated surfaces one or other of the preparations on the market that help to render chromium-plate impervious to moisture—and so to reduce tarnishing.

Norton Villiers Ltd. recommend using "Tekall", obtainable in ½ pt and 1 pt tins at most garages and accessory dealers. A soft rag soaked in "Tekall" should be wiped over the chromium-plated parts. This will leave an almost invisible film which is impervious to moisture.

**Keep All Nuts and Bolts Tight.** Occasionally (say, once a month) check over all external nuts and bolts for tightness (*see* page 61). Pay special attention to all drain plugs, the nuts securing the exhaust system, all control-lever clip bolts, the wheel-spindle nuts, the nuts at the base of the fork sliders, the brake-cam spindle nuts, the footrest hanger nuts, the screws securing the handlebars, the mudguard-securing nuts, and the small screw securing the headlamp front. Also keep a watchful eye on the rear chain spring-link, and the caps for the tyre inflation-valves.

## TYRES AND WHEEL ALIGNMENT

**Check Inflation Pressures Weekly.** Even the best quality rubber is not entirely impervious to air leakage, and tyre inflation pressures slowly but surely decline in spite of the fact that the tyres and valves are in perfect condition. Therefore check the inflation pressures of both tyres weekly, not by "thumbing" the covers or kicking them, but by using a suitable pressure gauge such as the Dunlop pencil-type No. 6, the Schrader No. 7750, the Romac, or the Holdtite. By maintaining the inflation pressures correct, tyre deflection is reduced to the minimum, and maximum comfort, tyre life, and freedom from skidding are assured. Avoid fierce braking and excessive acceleration. Also keep oil off the treads, and maintain the wheels in true alignment.

**Correct Inflation Pressures.** If you ride solo and are of normal weight, you should maintain the inflation pressures of the front and rear tyres at 18 lb per sq in. and 22 lb per sq in. respectively. If you are not of normal weight, carry heavy equipment, or a pillion passenger, it is necessary to

**MINIMUM TYRE INFLATION PRESSURES**

(Showing load per tyre and recommended pressure in lb per sq in.)

| Load | Pressure | Load | Pressure |
|---|---|---|---|
| 200 lb | 16 lb | 350 lb | 24 lb |
| 240 lb | 18 lb | 400 lb | 28 lb |
| 280 lb | 20 lb | 440 lb | 32 lb |

adjust the inflation pressures accordingly. Above are tabulated the correct minimum inflation pressures for specified loads per tyre.

The most satisfactory method of determining the correct inflation pressures required is to ride or take the machine to the nearest weighbridge and check individually the fully-laden weight on the front and rear tyres. Then consult the above table for the front and rear correct minimum inflation pressures. A suitable weighbridge is to be found at most large railway stations and other transport depots. The rider and pillion rider (if carried) must, of course, be seated.

**Checking Wheel Alignment (Solo).** To check the alignment on a solo machine, a straight-edge or a plain board (with one edge planed perfectly straight and square) about 5 ft long is required. Alternatively use a taut piece of string anchored at one end.

Jack up the motor-cycle on its stand, with the front and rear wheels parallel to each other. Then check the wheel alignment by holding the straight-edge, board, or string in contact with both tyres (about 4 in. above the ground and parallel with it). It should contact the front and rear of each tyre if the wheels are correctly aligned. This applies, of course, only to models having identical-section front and rear tyres. Where a front tyre of smaller section is fitted, check that the gaps between the straight-edge (or string) and the tyre sides are equal, front and rear. If the wheels are out of alignment, rectify matters by means of the adjusters screwed into the rear-fork ends (*see* page 103). Always check the wheel alignment after adjusting the secondary chain or altering the position of the rear wheel.

**Checking Wheel Alignment (Sidecar).** Two plain boards about 5 ft long are required. Each board must have one true edge. In addition, a third board of similar type, but about 4 ft long, is needed.

Before checking the wheel alignment of a sidecar outfit, place the outfit on a smooth floor, preferably a concrete surface. Referring to Fig. 47, to check that all three wheels of the outfit are running in track, place one of the long boards alongside the front and rear tyres of the motor-cycle and verify that the board contacts the front and rear of each tyre, as when checking alignment on a solo machine. Move the handlebars until the best contact is obtained.

Without disturbing the board placed alongside the motor-cycle tyres, place the second long board so that its true edge contacts the sidecar tyre, as illustrated in Fig. 47. Then, with a steel measuring tape, check dimensions *A* and *B*, with the tape as close to the tyres as practicable. To obtain

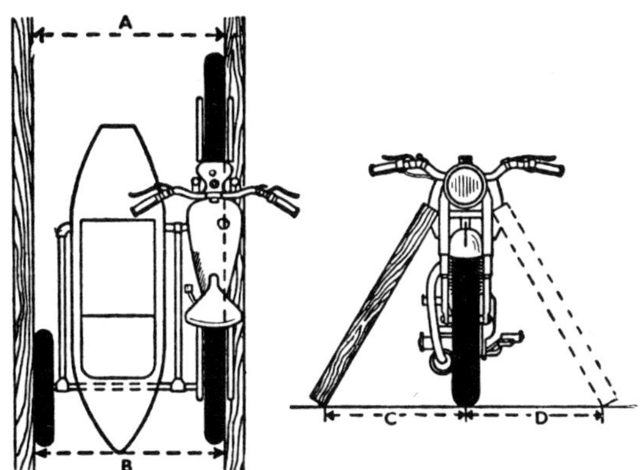


Fig 47 Checking wheel alignment on a sidecar outfit

*If alignment is correct, dimension A is about $\frac{3}{4}$ in. less than dimension B and dimension C slightly more than dimension D (see text).*

the best results, dimension *A* should be about $\frac{3}{4}$ in. less than dimension *B*. If the motor-cycle and sidecar wheels are dead parallel, there is a tendency for the sidecar outfit to pull towards the left. Some "toe-in" is necessary.

Having checked the three wheels for alignment, see whether the motor-cycle *leans slightly outwards*. Referring to Fig. 47, take the 4 ft board and rest it at a given point against the upper part of the telescopic front forks. Mark the floor where the edge of the board touches it. Then rest the board on the opposite side of the forks with its upper end in exactly the corresponding position and again mark the floor where the lower edge of the board touches. With the steel measuring-tape, check dimensions *C* and *D*. If the the machine is truly vertical, these two dimensions are equal. If the motor-cycle leans *outwards* the correct amount, dimension (*C*) should be about 1 in. more than dimension (*D*). To prevent drag on any right-hand bends the sidecar axle should be about 1 in. in front of the rear-wheel spindle. Follow exactly the sidecar maker's advice when fitting a sidecar.

The sidecar chassis fittings on a new outfit sometimes take a permanent "set," causing the motor-cycle to lean slightly towards the sidecar. This must be rectified by adjusting the attachment arms.

**Examine Cover Treads Occasionally.** It is a good plan occasionally to jack-up both wheels and carefully inspect the cover treads for small stones or flints which should be removed. Fill up cuts with some stopping compound. When fitting covers always remember that wired-on type beads are non-stretchable, also the valve is mid-way between them.

## BRAKES

**Ease of Brake Adjustments.** On all these models it is easy to keep the brakes highly efficient, because several means of adjustment are provided. It is possible to—

1. Adjust the position of the rear-brake pedal to suit individual requirements.
2. Make a minor hand adjustment of both brakes.

On 1955–63 models a thrust-pin adjustment for the brake shoes is also provided. Badly worn linings should always be renewed.

**To Adjust Brake Pedal (1955).** If the existing position of the rear-brake pedal on your machine does not suit you, it is possible to vary the pedal position within narrow limits (*see* Fig. 48) by means of the adjuster bolt (4) screwed into the heel of the pedal and secured by the lock-nut (5).

If it is desired to raise permanently the toe end of the pedal, *unscrew* the adjuster bolt (4) after first loosening the lock-nut (5). The best adjustment for normal purposes is to set the adjuster bolt so that, with the foot clear of the pedal, the arm of the brake pedal just clears the underside of the footrest arm.

Altering the position of the brake pedal necessarily moves the rear-brake rod (3) and therefore makes it necessary to check and if necessary alter the adjustment of the rear brake as described below.

**To Adjust Brake Pedal (1956–66).** On the 1956–65 models the rear-brake pedal is located by a spring-loaded sprag which is positioned between the stop on the pedal and the leg of the spring which is of the hairpin type and fitted to the inner side of the pedal boss.

To adjust the position of the brake pedal, first loosen the nut on the off-side of the pedal spindle. Then move the pedal to the best position (normally such that the pedal just clears the footrest rubber when the brake is off). Afterwards retighten securely the spindle nut. After altering the brake pedal position adjust the rear brake and re-set the stop-lamp which is adjustable.

**Adjusting the Rear Brake.** It is advisable to check the rear-brake adjustment occasionally. Unless considerable wear of the brake-shoe linings has taken place, it is generally found that only a minor brake adjustment is called for. The adjustment is correct when the brake-shoe linings are almost in contact with the rear brake drum when the pedal is in the "Off" position.

To make a rear brake adjustment, jack the machine up on its centre stand. Then on 1955 models to eliminate "lost motion," screw the hand adjuster (2) at the rear of the brake rod (*see* Fig. 54) farther on to the rod until slight friction is felt between the brake linings and the brake drum when the rear wheel is spun with the gear-change lever in "neutral." Having obtained contact between the linings and drum, *unscrew* the self-locking adjuster nut *two complete turns*.

On 1956–66 "swinging arm" models the rear-brake adjustment is similar to that just described for the 1955 models, but on the 1956–63 models the hand-type adjuster is on the front end of the brake rod (*see* Fig. 50). It is advisable after tightening the adjuster so that the brake linings just contact the drum, to *unscrew* the self-locking adjuster nut *five complete turns*.

Where it is not possible to adjust the rear brake by means of the hand adjustment, owing to a poor angle between the brake expander lever and rod, it is satisfactory (if the brake linings are serviceable) to make a brake shoe adjustment (*see* below).

**Adjusting the Front Brake.** This adjustment, like that of the rear brake, should be checked occasionally. It is satisfactory when the brake-shoe linings are nearly in contact with the front brake drum when the handlebar lever is not operated. Unless considerable wear of the brake linings, or of the cable control (or of both) develops, a minor hand adjustment should be sufficient. This is effected in the following manner—

The adjustment for the front brake is usually on the near-side of the telescopic-fork assembly. First jack up the machine on both its stands (on the centre stand on 1956 and subsequent models). Then slacken the knurled lock-nut. Now take up "lost motion" by unscrewing the knurled cable-adjuster nut until the brake-shoe linings just contact the brake drum when the front wheel is spun by hand. Finally, screw down the knurled adjuster *two complete turns* and tighten the lock-nut securely.

If hand adjustment of the front brake is no longer possible owing to the poor angle between the brake expander-lever and the cable, a major adjustment must be made by means of the brake shoes on 1955–63 models.

**Brake Shoe Adjustment (1955–63 Models).** After a very considerable mileage continuous adjustment of the hand adjuster for the front-brake cable or rear-brake rod causes the brake cam to become positioned so that

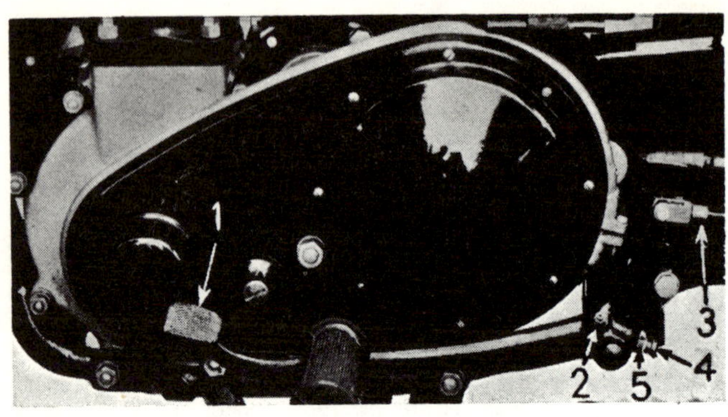


Fig 48 Adjustment for rear-brake pedal (1955)

*Note the detachable domed clutch-cover fitted in 1955–7 models.*

1. *Rear-brake pedal*
2. *Grease nipple*
3. *Rod to shoe expander-lever*
4. *Pedal adjuster-bolt*
5. *Lock-nut for item 4*

the available leverage is considerably reduced, causing a serious loss in brake efficiency. To remedy this it is necessary to make a shoe adjustment. A hardened and detachable thrust pin is fitted to one end of each brake shoe and shims can be fitted beneath the thrust pin as and when required, thereby increasing the effective height of the pin and compensating for brake lining wear.

Referring to Fig. 52, it is necessary only to remove the thrust pin (1) from the brake shoe (3) and then fit a shim washer (2) beneath the hardened thrust-pin. Eight shim washers (Part No. 000174) are available from the makers.

Having effected a brake shoe-adjustment, slacken off the hand adjuster and make the required brake-adjustment as described on page 97. See that the adjustment is not too close. The wheel must be able to turn without any friction.

**Interchangeability of Brake Shoes.** Although it is permissible to fit the rear-brake shoes and springs to the front brake cover-plate, this is not desirable without good reason. The brake shoes on the *same* cover-plate are *not* interchangeable.

**Positioning of Front Brake Cover-plate (1955–63).** The front brake cover-plate is secured to the front-wheel spindle with an internal and an external nut.

Fig 49 Secondary chain and brake adjustment on 1955 spring-frame Nortons

*A. Hub-spindle nut*
*B. Drawbolt-adjuster nut*
*C. Drawbolt-adjuster lock-nut*
*D. Drawbolt*
*E. Brake-rod adjuster nut*

*Later models replace drawbolts by screws.*

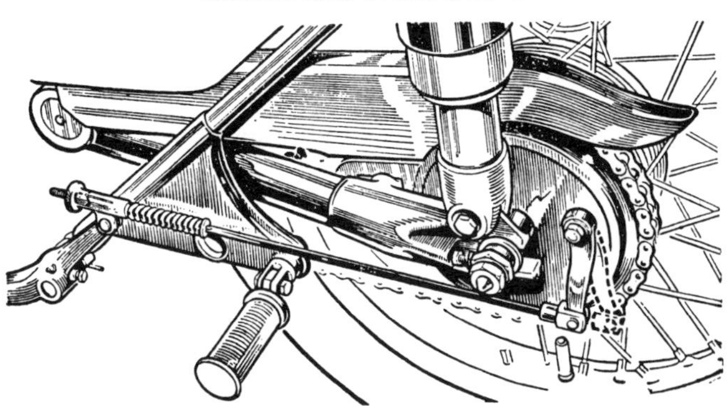

Fig 50 Rear brake adjustment on 1956–63 models

*Where the brake-rod adjustment is exhausted as shown, a brake-shoe adjustment is needed. On 1955, 1964–6 models the rod adjuster is at rear.*

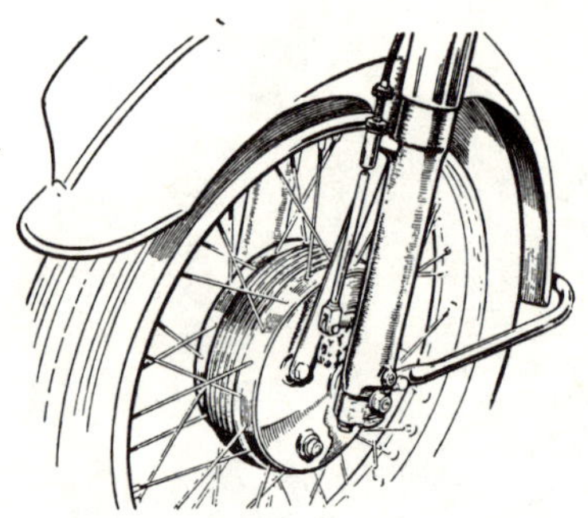

Fig 51 Front brake adjustment on 1955–63 models

*On 1964–6 models is a similar type of adjustment is provided, but on the 350 c.c. model it is on the off-side of the machine lower down. Where the cable adjuster thread is exhausted as shown above it is desirable on 1955–63 models to make a brake shoe thrust-pin adjustment.*

If the front wheel has been removed (*see* page 119), it is important, before replacing it in the "Teledraulic" front forks, to position the internal nut correctly.

On 1955–63 models position the internal nut so that when the cover-plate is applied, the outer face of the plate is flush with the edge of the wheel-hub shell.

Fit the external nut so that its hexagonal side abuts the front brake cover-plate.

**Centralize the Brake Shoes.** Where a front or rear brake cover-plate has been removed and the shoe assembly dismantled or disturbed, it is advisable to centralize the two shoes in the brake drum during assembly. This ensures that equal pressure is exerted on the drum by *both* linings. Lack of centralizing is often accompanied by an irritating squeak occurring during brake application.

Centralize the brake shoes before replacing the front wheel, or, where the rear wheel is concerned, after replacing the rear wheel.

To effect centralizing, first loosen the nut securing the brake cover-plate to the spindle of the wheel. Also (on 1955 and subsequent models) loosen slightly the nut on the fulcrum stud for the front wheel. Next increase the leverage of the shoe expander operating-lever by slipping a box spanner over the lever. Exert pressure on the spanner to expand the shoes to their full extent and simultaneously tighten the nut on the spindle so as to secure the brake cover-plate to the spindle. Also tighten (1955 onwards) the nut on the fulcrum stud for the front wheel.

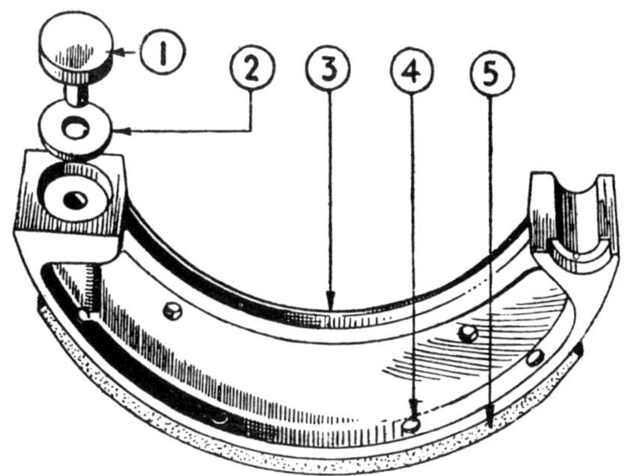


Fig 52 A.J.S./Matchless 1955–63 brake shoe with thrust-pin adjustment

1. *Hardened thrust-pin*
2. *Shim washer*
3. *Brake shoe*
4. *Rivet (8 per set) for securing lining*
5. *Brake-shoe lining*

## THE TRANSMISSION

**Maintenance of Four-speed Gearbox.** Apart from attending to lubrication as described on page 21 in Chapter 2, the gearbox itself needs no attention for thousands of miles. After a very big mileage it may need stripping-down and thoroughly overhauling. The gearbox is best returned to the makers or an authorized repairer for this work.

All 1955–6 models have a four-speed Burman gearbox and multi-plate clutch. On 1957–66 models a gearbox designed and made by Associated Motor Cycles, Ltd., is fitted. This compact unit incorporates some well-proved Norton features, and the clutch centre embodies a transmission shock-absorber of the rubber-block and vane type.

**Primary Chain Tension (1955–66).** The tension of the primary chain (*see* Figs. 57, 58) should be checked occasionally and, if necessary, adjusted. Adjustment of this chain must always be effected *before* that of the secondary chain, as it alters the tension of the secondary chain automatically.

To check the adjustment, place the machine on the centre stand and remove the inspection cap from the oil-bath chain case (*see* page 23). Then with the fingers check the chain whip (total up-and-down movement) mid-way between the two sprockets, with the chain in its tightest position. The whip should be approximately $\frac{3}{8}$ in.

**Primary Chain Adjustment 1955 Models.** If an adjustment is needed, slacken the nut on the right-hand side of the gearbox upper fixing bolt. Also loosen a few (2–3) turns the front nut on the gearbox adjuster eye-bolt. Then screw up the rear nut on the adjuster eye-bolt until the chain is felt to be quite taut, as checked with the fingers inserted through the inspection cap orifice. Now loosen the rear nut on the adjuster eye-bolt and carefully tighten the front nut to lock the assembly. Afterwards tighten the nut on the gearbox top fixing-bolt. Replace the inspection cap on the oil-bath chain case, and check the tension of the secondary chain.

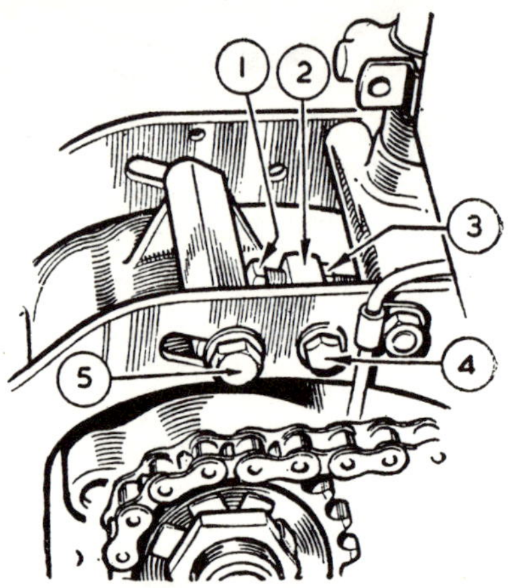


Fig 53 Primary chain adjustment on 1956–66 models

*The snap-on cover has been removed to show the adjustment.*

**Primary Chain Adjustment (1956–66).** On 1956–65 models a snap-on cover between the rear engine-plates gives instant access to a redesigned adjustment. Referring to Fig. 53, if a primary chain adjustment is called for, first loosen the nut on bolt 5 and also slacken lock-nut 3. Now screw the adjuster bolt 1 *into* the crosshead 2 to take up primary-chain slackness. Then pull on the secondary chain so as to to move the gearbox and tighten the primary chain until it is correctly tensioned (⅜ in. whip), as checked with the fingers through the inspection-cap hole on the oil-bath chain case. If the chain is over-tightened, screw the adjuster bolt 1 *out of* the cross-head 2.

After correctly retensioning the primary chain, retighten lock-nut 3 and also the nut on bolt 5. Finally replace the inspection cap on the oil-bath chain case, replace the snap-on cover over the engine plates, and check and if necessary adjust the tension of the secondary chain.

**Secondary Chain Adjustment (1955–66 Spring-frame Models).** Occasionally check that the tension of the secondary chain is correct. With the machine *on its centre stand* there should be 1⅛ in. total up-and-down movement at the centre of the lower chain run, with the chain in its tightest position. This whip is reduced to about ½ in. when the rider is seated and the wheels are resting on the ground.

Where a fully enclosed chain case (an optional extra) is fitted remove the rubber grommet in the case to check the chain tension. Note that where the secondary chain is fully enclosed the maintenance of correct chain tension is particularly important, otherwise the chain is likely to make contact with the chain case.

Before making an adjustment of the secondary chain, always check and if necessary adjust the tension of the primary chain (*see* page 102). After adjusting the secondary chain always check the rear-brake adjustment (*see* page 97).

On 1955 and later models an adjuster screw and lock-nut (*see* Fig. 54) are provided on the front side of each rear fork-end. To make a secondary chain adjustment (with the machine on its centre stand), loosen the spindle-end nut (3) on the near side; slacken the adjacent lock-nut (4) for the brake drum dummy spindle. Now loosen the lock-nut (6), on each side of the hub, and screw *out* the chain adjuster-screw (5) as required to tighten the chain correctly. Note that it is essential to unscrew both chain adjuster-screws *the same amount*, and before tightening the lock-nuts and spindle-end nut it is desirable to check the alignment of the wheels (*see* page 94).

**To Remove Secondary Chain (1955 Onwards).** On 1955 and later spring-frame models the guard for the secondary chain shrouds the chain very closely and the procedure outlined below is recommended if you wish to remove the chain without first removing the chain guard.

Position the motor-cycle on its centre stand and rotate the rear wheel until the connecting-link on the chain is close to the rear wheel sprocket. Remove the link. Now pass a piece of string (about 10 ft long) through the centre hole of the end link of the top run. Draw both ends of the string together and tie them together. Keeping the string taut at the rear end with one hand, with the other hand pull the bottom run of the chain backward. When the end of the top run of the chain leaves the gearbox sprocket the string will be left attached, one strand lying on each side of the sprocket teeth. When the chain is finally clear, cut the string on one side at a position approximately 1 ft from where it is looped through the chain link. Pending the replacement of the secondary chain, leave the string in position.

**To Replace Secondary Chain (1955 Onwards).** Push the longer cut end of the above-mentioned string through the hole in the centre of the chain end-link and tie both of the lower ends of the string together. Pull the string from the rear end, while guiding the chain up on to the gearbox sprocket teeth. Keep pulling until the chain encircles the rear-wheel sprocket. Afterwards remove the string and replace the chain connecting-link. Be careful when doing this to fit the spring link correctly (*see* Fig. 60).

Fig 54 Rear brake adjustment (1955) and secondary chain adjustment (1955 onwards) on Spring-frame models

1. *Grease nipple for brake-expander bush*
2. *Hand adjuster for rear brake (at front of rod, 1956 models)*
3. *Spindle-end nut*
4. *Lock-nut (brake cover-plate)*
5. *Chain adjuster-screw*
6. *Lock-nut for screw 5*

**Adjusting Dynamo Chain (1955–7).** The tension of the chain which drives the dynamo (*see* Fig. 57) should be checked *monthly* and adjusted if necessary in accordance with the instructions given on page 48 of Chapter 4. It is not necessary to remove the oil-bath chain case cover as shown in Fig. 57.

**Transmission Harshness (1955–6).** If harshness in the transmission develops, immediately check the level of oil in the oil-bath chain case. Provided the oil level is maintained correct, proper lubrication of the faces of the two cams of the shock-absorber (*see* Fig. 51) fitted to engine shaft is ensured. Top-up the oil level, using engine oil, as required (*see* page 20). If harshness continues, remove the outer half of the oil-bath chain case, and dismantle and lubricate the components of the shock-absorber.

When assembling the engine shaft shock-absorber, fit the components in this order: (*a*) the spacing collar, which is a sliding fit on the driving-side flywheel main-shaft and lies between the bearing of this shaft and the engine sprocket; (*b*) the engine sprocket, which is integral with the dynamo driving sprocket; (*c*) the shock-absorber cam which overrides the engine sprocket cam under the influence of the engine impulses (*d*) the shock-absorber spring; (*e*) the cap washer, which retains the shock-absorber spring; (*f*) the sleeve lock-nut, which must be firmly tightened against the driving side flywheel main shaft.

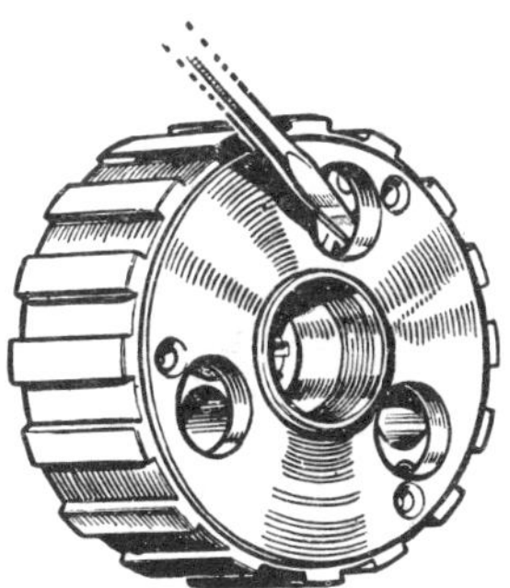

Fig 55 Showing (left) view inside the clutch shock-absorber compartment after removing three screws and prising off the steel cover-plate as shown (right)

**The Clutch Shock-absorber (1957–66 Models).** The 1957–66 engines do not incorporate an engine shaft shock-absorber, but instead a transmission shock-absorber embodied in the clutch centre. As may be seen in Fig. 55, the clutch shock-absorber has six rubber blocks. After a very considerable mileage it may become necessary to remove and renew these.

To remove the six rubber blocks, first remove the domed clutch-cover (1957 models) from the oil-bath chain case, or the oil-bath chain case cover (1958–66 models). Also remove the clutch spring pressure-plate (*see* Fig. 56), the springs, and the spring cups. Next remove the three securing-screws and prise off the steel cover-plate from the clutch shock-absorber compartment. Then remove the rubber blocks.

To compress the thick rubbers while extracting the thinner ones, a useful tool is a "C"-shaped spanner (engaging two slots in the clutch centre), having an extension handle fitted to it. To use this tool, engage fourth gear, apply the rear brake, position the tool, and pull the handle upwards (opposite to the direction of clutch rotation). Then with a short piece of hub spoke (pointed at the end), prise out the thin rubber blocks, followed by the thicker ones. Fit new rubber blocks in the reverse order of removal. Note that, where the clutch centre is removed, it is necessary to use a tool such as a gearbox main-shaft to hold the clutch centre while extracting the rubber blocks.

**Clutch Slip.** This must be avoided at all costs, as it causes damage and overheating, and spoils performance. Sometimes it is due to incorrect adjustment of the clutch springs (*see* page 108), but generally it is due to insufficient free movement in the clutch operating mechanism, which can be felt at the clutch lever. A method of testing for clutch slip is to place the machine on its stand, start up the engine, engage top gear, and then apply the rear brake. It should be possible to pull up the engine, even on full throttle, without the occurrence of clutch slip.

**Clutch Adjustment (1955–6).** With the clutch correctly adjusted there should be $\frac{1}{8}$–$\frac{3}{16}$ in. free movement of the clutch operating-cable. To check this free movement, lift the outer casing of the cable at the point where it enters the adjuster screw on the kick-starter casing cover, and see if you can move the casing freely with the fingers up-and-down the above amount. Also check backlash at the handlebar lever.

Should there be excessive free movement of the clutch control cable (resulting in clutch drag and noisy gear changing), adjust the clutch control in the following manner. First slacken the lock-nut on the clutch cable adjuster-screw and screw in the adjuster screw as far as possible to ensure that the internal operating lever is in its normal position. Next remove the domed clutch cover which is secured by eight screws.

With the plug spanner, slacken the large central lock-nut, and with a screwdriver gently screw in the thrust cup to which the lock-nut is fitted, until contact with the thrust rod (inside the gearbox mainshaft) can be felt. Then unscrew the thrust cap *exactly one-half turn*. Afterwards firmly retighten the central lock-nut. When doing this be careful not to allow the thrust cup to turn. Replace the domed clutch-cover and effect the final adjustment by unscrewing the external cable adjuster-screw until the correct amount of free movement of the clutch cable-casing ($\frac{1}{8}$–$\frac{3}{16}$ in.) is obtained. Finally secure the adjuster screw by tightening the lock-nut.

If insufficient free movement of the clutch cable (caused by wear of the friction inserts) is present, clutch slip results and an immediate adjustment must be made. Slacken off the external cable-adjuster, remove the domed clutch-cover, loosen the large central lock-nut, and then unscrew the thrust cup (to which the nut is fitted) a turn or two. Afterwards screw in the thrust cup until, as previously mentioned, the cup makes contact with the thrust rod inside the gearbox mainshaft. Then unscrew the thrust cup *exactly one-half turn*, and retighten the lock-nut. Finally replace the domed clutch-cover and make a control cable adjustment by means of the external screw and lock-nut until the required free movement of $\frac{1}{8}$–$\frac{3}{16}$ in. is obtained.

**Clutch Adjustment (1957–66).** All 1957–66 Matchless models have a four-speed gearbox and multi-plate clutch made by Associated Motor Cycles, Ltd. Details of the clutch and the clutch operating-mechanism

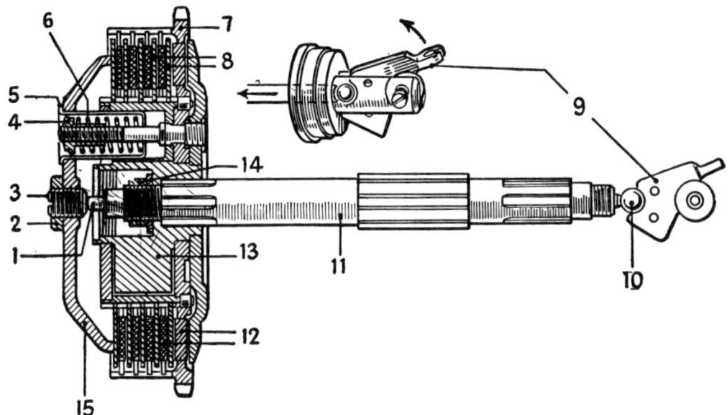


Fig 56 Details of Matchless multi-plate clutch and operating mechanism. Also fitted to late Norton

1. *Long thrust-rod*
2. *Lock-nut for 3*
3. *Adjustable thrust-cup*
4. *Spring adjusting-nut*
5. *Clutch-spring cup*
6. *Clutch spring (three)*
7. *Clutch sprocket*
8. *Steel plain-plates*
9. *Clutch operating-lever*
10. *Steel ball*
11. *Gearbox mainshaft*
12. *Friction-insert plates*
13. *Clutch centre*
14. *Nut securing 13*
15. *Spring pressure-plate*

are shown in Fig. 56. To avoid clutch slip or drag (caused by insufficient or excessive free movement of the cable), it is essential to maintain $\frac{1}{8}$–$\frac{3}{16}$ in. free movement of the clutch operating-cable.

Note that *insufficient* free movement will quickly ruin the clutch inserts and can generate sufficient heat to soften the clutch springs. Should clutch slip occur, make an *immediate* check of the free movement. *Excessive* free movement of the cable, besides causing clutch drag, also causes noisy gear changing.

To check for the correct free movement of the clutch operating-cable, lift the outer casing where it enters the adjustable cable-stop on the cover of the kick-starter casing. Total up-and-down movement should be as previously stated.

To rectify *insufficient* free movement of the operating cable (caused by wear of the friction inserts causing the plates to close up), first loosen the lock-nut and slacken off the adjustable cable-stop on the cover of the kick-starter casing. Next remove (1957 models) the domed cover (secured by eight screws) from the oil-bath chain case (Fig. 48). On 1958 and later models remove the screwed cap from the oil-bath chain case cover.

Referring to Fig. 56, with the sparking-plug spanner provided in the tool kit, loosen the lock-nut (2). Then with a screwdriver *unscrew* the thrust cup (3) a turn or two, and afterwards carefully screw it in until you feel it contacts the end of the long thrust-rod (1). Having done this, *unscrew* the thrust cup (3) *exactly one-half* turn, retighten the lock-nut (2), and screw home firmly the domed clutch-cover (1957) or screwed cap (1958–65). Finally adjust the cable stop until the required free movement ($\frac{1}{8}$–$\frac{3}{16}$ in.) of the operating cable is obtained, and retighten the cable stop lock-nut. Check for backlash at the clutch lever.

To rectify *excessive* free movement of the clutch operating cable, loosen the lock-nut on the adjustable cable-stop and, referring to Fig. 56, screw in the stop as far as possible to ensure that the operating lever (9) is in its normal position. Next slacken the lock-nut (2). With a screwdriver gently *screw in* the thrust cup (3) until you feel that it contacts the end of the long thrust rod (1). Then *unscrew* the thrust cup *exactly one-half turn* and finally retighten the lock-nut (2), taking care that the adjustable thrust cup does not also rotate. Refit the domed clutch cover on the oil-bath chain-case and make the final adjustment by the adjustable cable-stop. When these operations have been carried out, and the clutch adjustment is found to be correct, the cable-stop lock-nut should be retightened.

**To Adjust Clutch Springs (1955–6 Models).** A spring adjustment may be necessary if clutch slip persists in spite of the free movement of the clutch cable being correct (*see* page 106). Remove the domed cover (secured by eight screws) from the oil-bath chain case (*see* Fig. 57). This gives access to the clutch-spring adjuster nuts shown at *P* in Fig. 59.

To make an adjustment on 1955–6 models, use the slotted screwdriver provided on one of the spanners in the tool kit. *Screw in fully each adjuster nut and then unscrew it exactly four turns.* Then check (*see* page 106) whether clutch slip still exists. Further tightening is undesirable, especially as this causes the clutch to be rather heavy to operate. Should tightening beyond the recommended amount be necessary in order to cure clutch slip, this indicates that: (*a*) the springs have lost their proper tension; or (*b*) the clutch inserts are worn so badly that they need renewal; or (*c*) the inserts have become impregnated with oil.

**To Adjust Clutch Springs (1957–66).** As on 1955–6 models, an adjustment may be required if clutch slip continues in spite of the adjustment of the control cable being correct (*see* page 106). To obtain access to the clutch-spring adjuster nuts, on 1957 models, remove the domed cover (secured by eight screws) from the oil-bath chain case. On 1958–66 models remove the outer half of the oil-bath chain case. Care must be taken when doing this.

Referring to Fig. 56, remove the spring adjusting nuts (4), withdraw the three springs (6), and the spring cups (5). Then check that the spring cups do *not* contact the holes machined in the steel plate for the clutch shock-absorber assembly (*see* Fig. 55). Contact is indicated by burrs formed on the cups. Remove any burrs with a fine file and apply a little graphite grease on the cups before replacing them.

**Removing Outer Half of Oil-bath Chain Case (1955–7).** Place a suitable receptacle beneath the oil-bath to receive the oil as it runs out. Remove the near-side footrest arm.

The next step is to remove the screw which binds the metal band at the rear of the oil-bath chain case, and detach the band. Take off the rubber oil-sealing band, and remove the nut and plain washer from the bolt projecting from the centre of the chain case. Finally withdraw the outer half of the chain case. This exposes the primary chain, clutch, dynamo chain, and engine shaft shock-absorber (*see* Fig. 57).

**Removing Outer Half of Oil-bath Chain Case (1958–66).** A very strong polished aluminium oil-bath chain case is fitted to the coil-ignition models. As may be seen in Fig. 58, the rotor of the Lucas design alternator is secured to the engine shaft and the stator is bolted to the outer half of the chain case. Attached to the stator is an important cable which passes through the inner half of the chain case. Care must be taken not to damage this cable.

Remove the snap-on cover between the rear engine plates and disconnect the three snap connectors. Also remove the near-side footrest. Unscrew the knurled adjuster nut from the rod operating the rear brake. To catch engine oil which will drain from the chain case when the outer half is removed, lay a suitable drip tray beneath the chain case. Now remove the drain plug and allow all the oil (12 ounces) in the chain case to drain off. Also unscrew the oil-bath inspection cap (*see* page 23), and remove the nut located in the centre of the outer half of the chain case. Then remove the 14 screws which secure the outer half of the chain case.

With the rear brake pedal depressed, withdraw the outer half of the chain case *squarely* so as to prevent damaging the stator windings. Also *be most careful not to impose any strain on the stator cable.* Thread each connector through the rubber grommet in the oil-bath chain case, one at a time.

**Replacing Outer Half of Oil-bath Chain Case (1955–7).** Check that the faces of both halves of the chain case are clean and that the rubber and metal bands are both clean and undamaged. The rubber band is of the endless type and of larger section than the earlier version. Position the outer half of the chain case so that its exterior edge coincides exactly with that of the back half, and then fit the endless rubber-band. Next fit the

Fig 57 Oil-bath chain case with outer half removed (1955–57)

*This view shows the engine shaft shock-absorber, the primary chain, the clutch, and the dynamo driving chain. The engine shaft shock-absorber is omitted on* 1958–66 *models (see page* 105).

metal band. Begin at the front end of the chain case and draw together the two free ends of the band with one hand, while inserting the binding screw with the other hand. When tightening the binding screw, apply light blows (with a rubber mallet) all round the exterior of the band. This will cause the metal band to creep on the rubber band and enable the binding screw to be fully tightened down. Replace the nut and washer on the centre fixing-bolt, replace the footrest arm and finally remove the inspection cap from the oil-bath chain case, pour in engine oil (page 22) to the correct level, and replace the inspection cap.

**Leakage from Oil-bath (1955–7).** If leakage be detected after replacing and replenishing the oil-bath chain case, this may be due to one or both faces of the case being damaged or distorted. Both faces should fit closely to a surface plate and, if there is any suspicion of distortion due to accidental impact prior to assembly, a check with a surface plate should be made. Another possible cause of oil leakage is imperfect registering of the two joint faces during assembly. Great care must be taken to ensure *exact* registering of the halves, without which an oil-tight oil-bath is unobtainable. It is also essential to see that the rubber band is correctly positioned, and that the contacting faces are scrupulously clean.

**Replacing Outer Half of Oil-bath Chain Case (1958 Onwards).** First check that the paper washer is undamaged. Offer up the outer half of the chain case and gently take up the slack of the stator lead (*see* Fig. 58) by

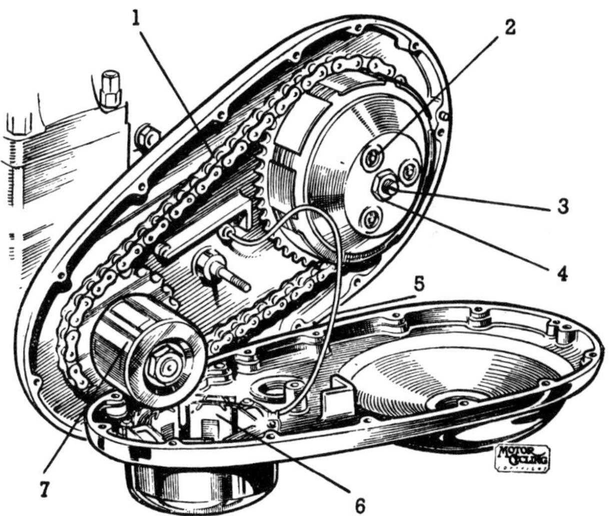


Fig 58 Oil-bath chain case with outer half removed (1958–66)

*No engine shaft shock-absorber is included, the transmission shock-absorber being included in the clutch.*

1. *Primary chain*
2. *Spring adjusting-nuts*
3. *Adjustable thrust cup*
4. *Lock-nut for 3*
5. *Stator lead*
6. *Stator*
7. *Rotor*

pulling on the lead from the back of the inner half of the chain case. Locate the outer half of the case with the central nut and tighten the nut lightly.

Replace the 14 securing screws and tighten them first in a diagonal order, and then all round the case. Now tighten firmly the central fixing nut, and replenish the oil-bath chain case with suitable engine oil to the correct level (*see* page 22). Finally replace the screwed inspection cap (*see* page 23), fit the rear-brake adjuster nut, and the near-side footrest, connect up the three snap connectors, and replace the snap-on cover between the rear engine plates.

**To Remove a Clutch Control Cable.** The following is the procedure for removing a clutch control cable where renewal is required. It applies to all 350 and 500 c.c. models. First remove the oil filler cap from the cover of the kick-starter case. Next screw home fully the clutch cable adjuster on top of the kick-starter case cover. Now disconnect the clutch cable inner wire from the clutch operating lever. This can be done through the oil filler cap orifice. Also disconnect the clutch inner wire from the clutch operating lever on the left-hand side of the handlebars. Then pull the cable lower end until it is clear of the motor-cycle. When doing this ease the cable through the frame cable clips.

**To Replace Clutch Cable.** Proceed in the reverse order of removal, and finally check and, if necessary, adjust the clutch operation as described on pages 106 onwards.

**To Remove Primary Chain and Clutch Assembly (1955–6).** The outer half of the oil-bath chain case must first be removed, as described on page 109. Referring to Fig. 59, remove by unscrewing uniformly (with end of spanner Part No. 017254) the four spring-adjustment nuts (*P*) and withdraw the clutch spring pressure-plate (*F*), complete with the four springs (*M*) and spring cups (*R*). Now remove the spring link from the primary chain and take the chain off the sprockets.

With top gear still engaged, again apply the rear brake and, after flattening the turned up part of the locking plate *W* located beneath the large central nut, unscrew the nut *V* retaining the clutch centre *E* to the sleeve on the gearbox mainshaft *T*. Remove the locking plate *W* and the plain washer *X* situated on the main-shaft behind the retaining nut. The entire clutch assembly may now be removed.

Withdraw the clutch assembly bodily by pulling it away from the gearbox mainshaft. The use of an extractor is generally quite unnecessary, as the clutch centre is a sliding fit on the mainshaft, but avoid losing any of the twenty-four clutch-bearing rollers which become free to move endwise when the clutch centre and sprocket assembly (including the roller bearing retaining-washers) is withdrawn from the mainshaft.

**To Remove Primary Chain and Clutch Assembly (1957–66).** First remove the outer half of the oil-bath chain case (page 109). Referring to Fig. 56, remove by unscrewing uniformly (with the end of spanner Part No. 017254) the spring adjusting-nut (4), and take away the spring pressure-plate (15), complete with the three clutch springs (6) and the clutch-spring cup (5). Disconnect the primary chain by removing the

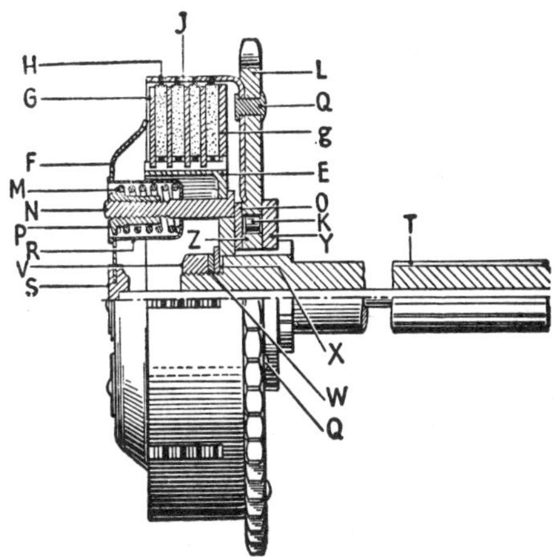


Fig 59 Details of 1955–6 Burman multi-plate clutch

E. *Clutch centre*
F. *Spring pressure-plate*
G,g. *Steel plain-plates*
H. *Friction plates (five, 500 c.c.)*
J. *Clutch case*
K. *Roller-bearing rollers (24)*
L. *Clutch sprocket*
M. *Clutch spring (four or five)*
N. *Stud for spring-adjustment nut*
O. *Washer (thin) retaining roller-bearing*
P. *Spring-adjustment nut*
Q. *Rivet*
R. *Spring cup (one of four)*
S. *Pressure-plate boss*
T. *Gearbox mainshaft*
V. *Nut retaining clutch-centre*
W. *Locking plate*
X. *Plain washer*
Y. *Washer (thick) retaining roller-bearing*
Z. *Roller-bearing ring*

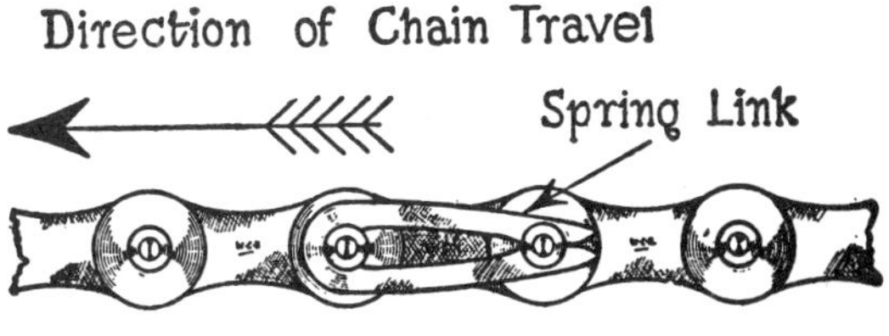

Direction of Chain Travel

Spring Link

Fig 60 Be careful to replace a chain spring-link correctly

*The closed end must always face the direction of chain movement.*

spring link, and remove the chain. Engage fourth gear and apply the rear brake. Then with a suitable box spanner unscrew the nut (14) which secures the clutch centre (13) to the gearbox mainshaft (11). Now pull away the complete clutch assembly from the mainshaft. An extractor is available if required.

**Replacing Clutch Centre, Clutch Sprocket, and Primary Chain (1955–6).** Referring to Fig. 59, fit the roller bearing retaining-washer (*Y*) on the gearbox mainshaft splined-sleeve. This is the thicker of the two retaining washers. Next replace the roller-bearing ring (*Z*) on the splined sleeve of the mainshaft and with thick grease position the twenty-four rollers (*K*) on the bearing ring. Replace the clutch sprocket (*L*) over the rollers.

Next fit to the gearbox mainshaft splined-sleeve the washer (*O*) retaining the roller bearing. This is the thinner of the two retaining washers. Then fit the clutch centre (*E*) to the splined sleeve of the mainshaft and push home. Afterwards replace in this order: the plain washer (*X*), the locking plate (*W*), and the nut (*V*) retaining the clutch centre. This nut cannot be fully tightened until the primary chain is fitted.

Replace the primary chain on the two sprockets, being careful that the spring link is correctly fitted (*see* Fig. 60). Now tighten very firmly the nut (*V*) which retains the clutch centre (*E*) to the mainshaft splined-sleeve. When tightening this nut, engage fourth gear and apply the rear brake to prevent the mainshaft turning. Turn up the edge of the locking plate (*W*) against a flat on the nut (*V*) retaining the clutch centre (*E*).

**Fitting Clutch Plates and Springs (1955–6).** Referring to Fig. 59, slide into position in the clutch case (*J*) attached to the clutch sprocket (*L*) a steel plain-plate (*g*). Make certain that the recessed part of this steel plate faces *towards* the clutch centre (*E*) and overhangs its flange (350 c.c. models).

Next slide into position one of the clutch friction-insert plates (*H*). Then fit a steel plain-plate, followed by another friction-insert plate, and so on, alternately, until the complete set of plates has been fitted. It should be noted that 350 c.c. models have five steel plain-plates and four friction-insert plates, whereas 500 c.c. models have six and five respectively.

Now insert the four spring cups (*R*) into the spring pressure-plate (*F*) and offer up the pressure plate to the assembly. Fit the clutch springs (*M*) and retain the springs in place by screwing the four adjusting nuts (*P*) on to the studs (*N*). Tighten each nut a few turns as fitted, and then fully tighten in a uniform manner all four nuts. Afterwards slacken back each adjustment nut *four complete turns*. This is the standard spring-adjustment.

Finally check the adjustment of the primary chain and replace the outer half of the oil-bath chain case (*see* pages 111 and 112). Also verify that there is sufficient free movement in the clutch control (*see* page 106).

**Replacing Clutch Centre, Clutch Assembly, and Primary Chain (1957–66).** Referring to Fig. 56, apply a little anti-centrifuge grease to the clutch-sprocket bearing, and position the complete clutch-assembly over the bearing rollers. (Note that if the clutch assembly has been removed from the clutch centre, fit first the clutch sprocket, and then alternately steel plain-plates and friction insert plates.) Then fit the spring washer and the nut (14) securing the clutch centre (13) to the gearbox mainshaft (11). Tighten this nut lightly. Replace the primary chain, being careful to see that its spring link is correctly fitted (*see* Fig. 60). Engage fourth gear, apply the rear brake, and then tighten firmly the nut (14) securing the clutch centre (13), to the mainshaft. Position the spring pressure-plate (15) and fit in this order: the clutch-spring cups (5), the three clutch springs (6), and the spring adjusting-nuts (4). With the end of the appropriate spanner (Part No. 017254), screw home the adjusting-nuts until they are *just flush with the spring cups*. Finally check the primary chain adjustment (*see* page 102), and the clutch control adjustment (*see* page 109). Replace the outer half of the oil-bath chain case (*see* page 110).

**To Remove Clutch Bearing (1957 Onwards).** The clutch centre is secured to the clutch back plate by the three clutch studs and lock-nuts. The bearing can be removed after separating the clutch centre from the back plate. Before assembling, apply a little anti-centrifuge grease.

**To Remove A.C. Rotor and Engine Sprocket (1958–66).** First remove the outer half of the oil-bath chain case (*see* page 109). With fourth gear engaged, connect the rear-brake rod to the brake pedal. Next exert pressure on the rear-brake pedal and unscrew the lock-nut and nut which secure the rotor to the engine shaft. Then remove the washer and pull off the rotor shown at (7) in Fig. 58. The rotor is keyed to the engine shaft. Remove the key for the rotor and also the distance piece ($\frac{13}{32}$ in. wide). The engine sprocket can now be removed. It is not necessary to remove the distance piece behind it.

## THE FRAME, ETC.

**To Check Steering Head Adjustment.** Jack up the front of the machine by placing a box beneath the crankcase to take all the weight off the front wheel. Then exert hand pressure upwards from the extreme ends of the handlebars. There should be no appreciable shake present and the steering head must be quite free to turn. If some shake is detected, adjust the steering head forthwith as described below.

**To Adjust Steering Head (1955–63).** The following is the correct procedure for adjusting the steering head. It is assumed that the front wheel is quite clear of the ground. Loosen the two pinch-screws in the fork crown. Next slacken the domed lock-nut at the top of the steering column. Having slackened the lock-nut, screw down very gradually the lower adjusting nut for the steering head. This adjusting nut is located immediately below the lock-nut and should be turned with an adjustable spanner. While tightening the lower adjusting nut, test for steering-head slackness by placing the fingers over the gap between the frame top-lug and the handlebar lug, while simultaneously exerting upward pressure on the front edge of the front mudguard.

Tighten the adjusting nut until the steering head is free to turn without perceptible up-and-down play. Afterwards tighten the domed lock-nut and the two pinch-screws in the fork crown. Finally withdraw the box or other packing from beneath the footrests.

**To Adjust Steering Head (1964–6).** On 350 and 500 c.c. models having "Roadholder" front forks the following are the correct instructions for adjusting the steering head. With the front wheel clear of the ground, referring to Fig. 61 first loosen the two nuts (10) on the pinch studs (11) for the fork crown lug. Also loosen slightly the fork crown and column lock-nut (6). Then with a thin open-ended spanner, $1\frac{3}{8}$ in. across the flats, adjust the steering head adjuster (8) as required. The bearings should have no play but free movement. When making an adjustment, check for bearing play by trying to raise or lower the front wheel with one hand while using the fingers of the other hand around the handlebar lug where it meets the frame. If play exists some movement can be felt. After eliminating all play, retighten the securing nuts (6) and (10). Note: when checking steering-head adjustment also check the fork filler plugs (7) for tightness.

**Maintenance of "Teledraulic" Front Forks.** Apart from checking the level of the hydraulic fluid every 5000 miles (*see* page 25) and topping-up if necessary, no attention is called for. No adjustment is necessary and all working parts are automatically lubricated by means of the hydraulic damping fluid. Unless damage has been accidentally sustained, the "Teledraulic" front forks should normally not require to be dismantled. However, after a very big mileage (say 30,000 miles) the oil seals and washers may require attention.

**The "Roadholder" Front Forks (1964–6).** Apart from draining and replenishing the fork legs with damping oil at long intervals (*see* page 27), no maintenance is necessary. All internal parts are automatically lubricated and unless the front forks are damaged in an accident they are unlikely to require to be dismantled. For this reason instructions on stripping down the forks and reassembling them have not been included in this handbook.

**"Swinging-arm" Rear Suspension.** As regards lubrication (*see* page 28), no attention should normally be required, except perhaps very occasionally on 1955–6 models with Matchless "Teledraulic" rear-suspension units, and then only if the telescopic legs become excessively lively.

On 1957–66 models (with Girling rear-suspension units) in the event of the legs becoming noisy in action, grease the outside of each spring as described on page 27. The springs on the Girling units are adjustable for loading. If you are above average weight, carry a pillion passenger, or regularly negotiate rough terrain, raise the base of each spring as required by turning with a "C" spanner *clockwise* the cam ring provided at the base of each telescopic lower member. Three positions are obtainable, and the highest gives the maximum stiffness of springing. The application of a little thin oil to the cam ring facilitates an adjustment. Should you fit a sidecar to your machine, it is advisable to change the suspension-unit springs, as stronger springs are generally desirable.

**Handlebar Adjustment.** The handlebars on the majority of 1955–66 models are adjustable for angle to suit individual requirements. Loosen the three securing screws and then adjust the handlebars as required.

After making the adjustment, be sure to retighten firmly the three securing screws.

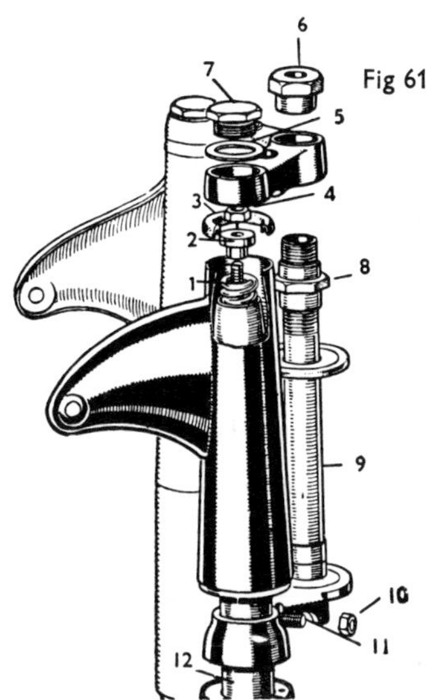


Fig 61 "Roadholder" front forks and the steering head adjustment (1964–6)

**KEY TO FIG. 61**

1. *Main spring*
2. *Main spring locating bush*
3. *Main tube top cover ring*
4. *Nut for top of damper rod*
5. *Washer for filler plug 7*
6. *Fork crown and column lock-nut*
7. *Filler plug*
8. *Steering head adjuster nut*
9. *Crown lug with column*
10. *Nut for stud 11*
11. *Pinch stud for crown lug*
12. *Fork main tube*

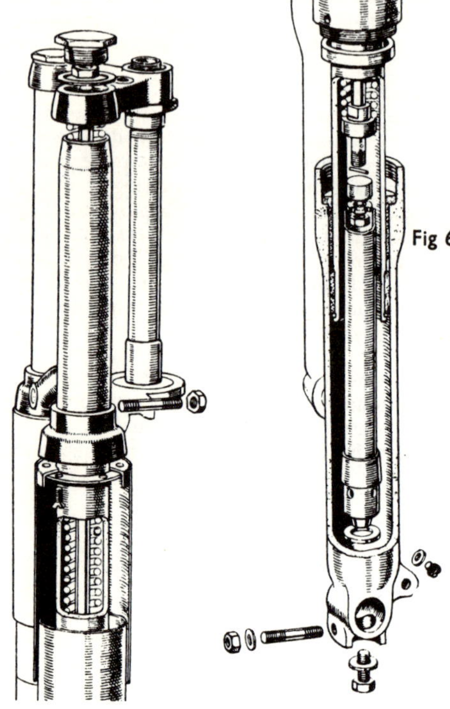

Fig 62 Telescopic front forks (1959 Norton), upper (left) and lower parts

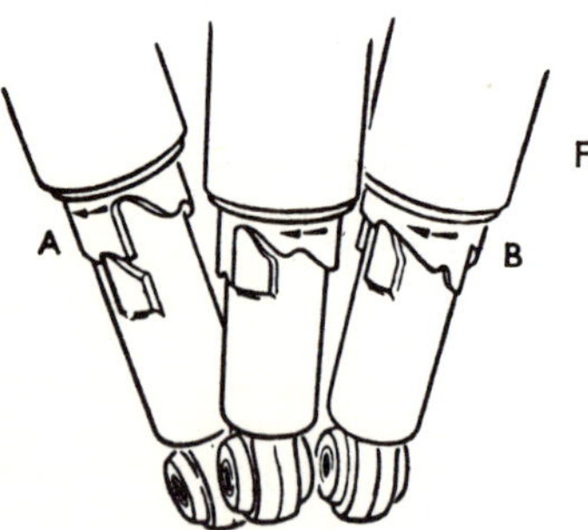


Fig 63 Showing the three settings for cam ring adjustment, 1957–66 Girling rear suspension units

*Positioning the cam ring as shown at A gives maximum stiffness of springing, and as shown at B the minimum stiffness of springing.*

## WHEEL REMOVAL

**To Remove the Front Wheel (1955–63).** Jack the machine up on its centre stand. Disconnect the yoke end of the front-brake cable from the brake-expander lever by removing the split pin and retaining pin. On 1955–63 models remove the bolt securing the brake anchor-stay to the brake cover-plate. Next loosen the nut on the left-hand side of the front-wheel spindle.

Remove the four nuts which clamp the fork-slider caps to the "Teledraulic" fork sliders. Detach both caps and place them aside separately, so that they may later be replaced exactly as prior to removal. These caps must *not* be interchanged. Apply pressure to the front wheel so as to reduce the effective height of the wheel spindle, and withdraw the wheel towards the front.

**Replacing the Front Wheel (1955–63).** Hold the left-hand fork-slider cap under the location on the front-wheel spindle, and offer up the front wheel assembly and cap so as to engage the cap with its two retaining studs.

When replacing the front wheel remember to apply pressure to flatten the tyre so as to enable the wheel spindle to pass between the forward studs securing the fork-slider caps. Fit the two nuts securing the near-side fork-slider cap and wheel spindle and tighten these nuts lightly. Then fit the off-side fork-slider cap and tighten lightly the cap securing-nuts. See that the fork-slider caps are not interchanged. Now attach firmly the brake anchor-stay to the cover plate, and replace the yoke end and pin.

Tighten lightly the nut on the near side of the front-wheel spindle. Then firmly and evenly tighten the two nuts which secure the near-side fork-slider cap. Verify that the gaps, fore and aft, between the cap and the end of the fork slider are *exactly* equal. Ensuring that these gaps are equal is very important. Now tighten firmly the nut on the near-side of the front-wheel spindle, and lastly the nuts securing the off-side slider cap.

**After Replacing Front Wheel (1955–63).** If any stiffness in the action of the telescopic front-forks is noticed after replacing the front wheel, slacken the nuts securing the off-side slider cap, operate the forks sharply up and down, and retighten the slider cap-securing nuts. This should cure the stiffness.

**To Remove Front Wheel (1964–6 Models).** First place the machine on its centre stand and remove the split pin and pin retaining the yoke end of the front-end cable to the brake-expander lever. Unscrew the off-side wheel spindle nut (R.H. thread) and loosen the pinch-stud nut on the near-side fork slider end.

Take the weight of the wheel in the left hand and withdraw the spindle from the near side by means of a tommy-bar placed through the hole in the head of the spindle. As the wheel is withdrawn take great care not to allow the brake plate to fall. If allowed to do so, the bevelled edge can be seriously damaged. Place the wheel spindle, brake plate, and dust cover in a clean receptacle to prevent contamination by grit.

**To Replace Front Wheel (1964–6 Models).** Reassemble in the reverse order of dismantling. Fit the brake plate to the brake drum and as the wheel is lifted into the "Roadholder" front forks, position the dust cover on the near-side and make sure that the torque stop on the brake plate engages the slot in the off-side leg.

Remove all traces of rust from the wheel spindle and grease the spindle. With the right hand pass the spindle through the hub and replace and tighten the off-side spindle nut. Deflect the telescopic forks several times to "centre" the near-side leg on the spindle. Do not overtighten the pinch-stud nut on the near-side fork slider end. The lug on the fork end can be broken if this stud is over tightened. Finally re-connect, adjust the brake cable. If fork stiffness develops after replacing the wheel, loosen the R.H. spindle nut, operate the forks up and down.

**Removing Quickly-detachable Rear Wheel (1955–63 Spring frame Models).** First place the motor-cycle on its centre stand. On 1955–8 models slacken the bolt located at the rear on each tubular member to which the detachable rear-portion of the mudguard is attached. Also loosen the two bolts holding the two portions of the mudguard together. Disconnect the snap connector provided in the lead to the stop-tail lamp. Now remove the detachable rear-portion of the rear mudguard.

On 1959–63 models a deep section *one-piece* mudguard is fitted. To facilitate rear wheel removal it is desirable to lay some suitable packing (e.g. wood blocks) beneath the centre stand so as to lift the rear wheel a greater distance from the ground.

Referring to Fig. 64, disconnect the speedometer drive by unscrewing the cable gland-nut (5) and withdrawing the end of the driving cable from the speedometer-drive gearbox (4). Do *not* loosen the nut which secures the speedometer gearbox. Next remove the nut (11) and washer (12) from the near side of the hub spindle (7). Do not disturb the nut (10) which secures the brake cover-plate. Withdraw the hub spindle (7), by means of its short tommy-bar, together with the distance collar (6), which will fall away as the spindle is withdrawn. Then ease the hub sideways from the drilled holes on the brake-drum wall (1955–6 models), or ease the rubber-sleeved pins on the hub from the tubular bosses on the brake-drum wall (1957–63 models). The rear wheel is then free to be withdrawn from the machine which should be leaned at an angle (1959–63 models).

**To Replace Quickly-detachable Rear Wheel (1955–63 Spring frame Models).** Follow the removal procedure in reverse. Referring to Fig. 64, offer up the quickly-detachable wheel, insert the hub spindle (7) *without* the distance collar (6); engage the holes or tubular bosses in the brake-drum wall, with the hub driving-pins; hold the wheel in its normal position;

withdraw the hub spindle. Then insert the distance collar and replace the hub spindle. When tightening the nut on the nearside of the spindle, make sure that the opposite end of the spindle contacts the secondary chain adjuster-screw, to ensure correct wheel alignment. This should be correct if the chain adjuster-screws have not been disturbed. If in any doubt, check the wheel alignment (*see* page 93); also check the adjustment of the rear brake; (*see* page 97).

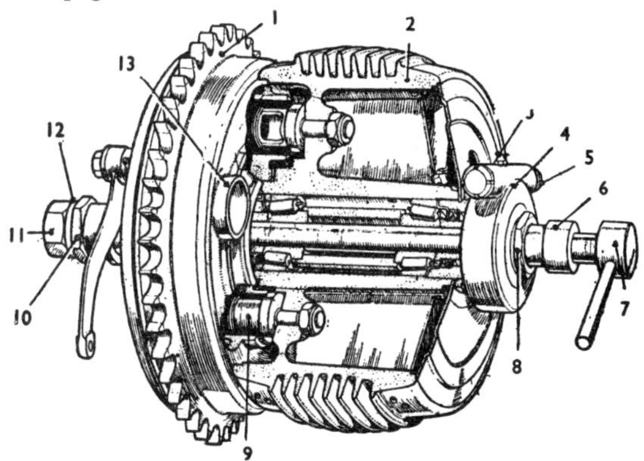


Fig 64 Details of light-alloy hub assembly on 1955–63 spring-frame models with quickly-detachable rear wheel

*On 1955–6 models the brake-drum wall has 'rilled holes instead of the bosses shown; these bosses engage rubber-sleeved pins on the light-alloy hub.*

1. *Brake drum and sprocket*
2. *Full-width light-alloy hub*
4. *Speedometer-drive gearbox*
5. *Gland nut for speedometer-drive cable*
6. *Distance collar*
7. *Hub spindle*
8. *Nut locating 4*
9. *Rubber-sleeved driving pins on 2*
10. *Nut securing brake cover-plate*
11. *Nut on spindle end*
12. *Washer for 11*
13. *Tubular bosses to engage pins 9*

*(By courtesy "Motor Cycle" London)*

When replacing the rear wheel, make sure that the speedometer-drive dogs engage properly before tightening the cable gland-nut (5). Defer tightening the nut (8) locating the speedometer-drive gearbox (4) until the driving cable has been connected up, and the hub-spindle nut (11) has been tightened. Also make sure that the brake cover-plate anchorage is correct (*see* Fig. 65).

**To Remove Quickly-detachable Rear Wheel (1964–6 Models).** Because a deep section one-piece rear mudguard is fitted it is desirable to lay some suitable packing (e.g. wood blocks) beneath the centre stand so as to lift the rear wheel a greater distance from the ground.

Remove the three rubber grommets from the off-side of the rear hub and then with a box or socket spanner remove the three sleeve nuts which secure the rear hub to the brake drum. Unscrew and remove the right-hand portion of the wheel spindle. Remove on the same side the distance piece and speedometer-drive gearbox, and allow the latter to hang on its cable. Now withdraw the rear hub from the driving studs on the brake drum by pulling it to the off-side. By inclining the machine the rear wheel can then be lifted clear of the motor-cycle.

If it is desired to remove the brake drum, take off the hand adjuster from the rear brake rod and remove the secondary chain. Then unscrew the nut securing the dummy spindle and pull clear the brake drum.

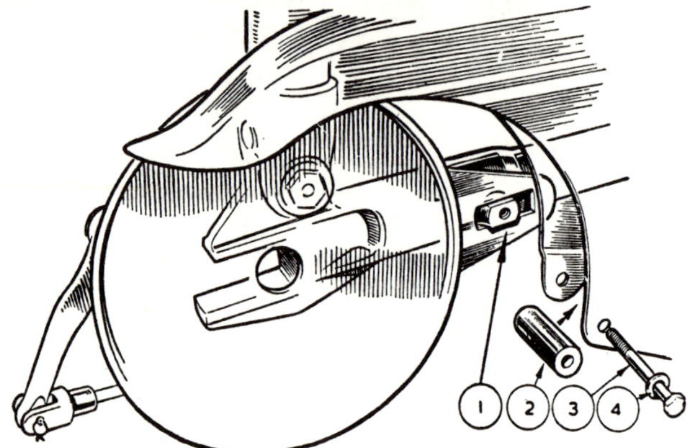


Fig 65 The rear brake cover-plate anchorage (1955–63 spring-frame models)

1. *Brake-anchorage boss*
2. *Distance sleeve*
3. *Anchorage bolt*
4. *Washer*

**To Remove Rear Wheel (Not Quickly-detachable Type).** First disconnect the rear brake rod by removing the split pin and yoke end pin. Also remove the connecting link of the secondary chain. Lay a sheet of paper beneath the chain to prevent its contamination with dirt. Next remove the bolt which passes through the rear brake anchor lug and the secondary chain guard. Be careful not to lose the distance piece between it and the chain guard.

Now disconnect the speedometer-drive cable from its drive. Loosen several turns the nut on the rear wheel spindle and pull the wheel to the off-side until the brake plate clears the anchor boss on the frame. Then remove the secondary chain from its sprocket and withdraw the rear wheel, inclining the motor-cycle at an angle to assist withdrawal under the silencer.

# Index